Discretion and Lawlessness: Compliance in the Juvenile Court

Discretion and Lawlessness: Compliance in the Juvenile Court

James T. Sprowls
The University of
Wisconsin—Milwaukee

LexingtonBooks
D.C. Heath and Company
Lexington, Massachusetts
Toronto

Library of Congress Cataloging in Publication Data

Sprowls, James T
Discretion and lawlessness

Bibliography: p.
Includes index.
1. Juvenile courts—United States. I. Title.
KF9794.S65 345.73'08 79-6735
ISBN 0-669-03540-8

Published simultaneously in Canada

Printed in the United States of America

International Standard Book Number: 0-669-03540-8

Library of Congress Catalog Card Number: 79-6735

Contents

List of Tables

Foreword

The rhetoric claiming that tyranny begins where law ends is excessive and ethnocentric. It is more accurate (but less stirring) to assert that tyranny is less likely with law than without it; and even this bland proposition is open to challenge. Societies exist in which the rule of law prevails in a draconian and repressive manner. Apartheid is tyrannical even though (perhaps especially because) it is codified in elaborate and precise statutory language.

As the existence of law does not guarantee justice, neither does its absence guarantee injustice. Mercy, for example, is the suspension of law in favor of charity. Can we say that judges who sometimes temper the harshness of statutory requirements are tyrants in a world long dominated by despotic kings, emperors, generalissimos, ayatollahs, fuhrers, and premiers?

If law itself can by tyrannical, and its absence a blessed relief, why is it that John Locke's dictum—"Wherever law ends, there tyranny begins"—is still stirring to libertarians who champion the causes of freedom and human dignity? It is because the phrase captures a fundamental truth: human affairs are more likely to be fairly and equitably regulated if principles prevail rather than the prejudices and preferences of judges. But principles can never prevail to the exclusion of preferences and prejudices. However desirable it may seem to live under a government of laws rather than of men, the reality that law is made and implemented by human beings cannot be escaped. As human behavior is too varied and quickly changing to be described, let alone regulated in detail by written documents, judgment will always be required of judges. Discretion begins where law ends. If it is argued that discretion (with its potential for arbitrary and capricious decision making) is a mild form of tyranny, then it can be countered that tyranny, like whiskey, may be beneficial in small doses.

As law without discretion cannot exist (except in philosophers' imaginations) then the practical problem is entirely a matter of dosage. How much discretion ought there to be? Even if agreement about this could be achieved, there is always the danger that discretion, like whiskey, can be addictive and corrupting. How can its use be controlled?

That is the subject of this book. James Sprowls presents an empirical study of the relationship between law and behavior in an area of judicial administration with a tradition of unbridled discretion in an age of legalistic reform.

The creation of juvenile courts represented a policy decision to suspend the rule of law in favor of a system of therapeutic discretion for children. Turn-of-the-century reformers, such as Jane Addams, Julia Lathrope, and Julian Mack, campaigned successfully for special children's courts in which procedural formality was abandoned to facilitate the diagnosis and treatment of maladjusted and deprived youngsters. Lawyers, juries, rules of evidence, even the requirement that guilt be convincingly proved were dispensed with so as to maximize the discretionary power of judges, who were expected not only to pursue justice and the protection of the public but also to act in the best interests of each individual delinquent.

Other twentieth-century American courts and administrative agencies have also been vested with great discretionary power, but none with the same wholesale abandonment of due process as the juvenile court nor with the same conviction that discretion was necessary for the socially desirable resolution of cases. Nor has any other agency of discretionary justice been subjected to more scathing denunciations in the past twenty years.

Current wisdom has it that the investiture of discretionary power in the juvenile court is too great. Criminological and popular literature attacking the administration of juvenile justice is abundant. It is said that serious offenders are left unpunished, petty offenders are often brutalized and made more antisocial, and the informal, "therapeutic" procedures of the juvenile court are quixotic and unfair.

As in so many areas of public life, the current era of reform was ushered in by the Warren Court. Noting that the condition of being a boy does not justify the use of kangaroo courts, the Supreme Court in a series of landmark decisions required an infusion of due-process safeguards into the juvenile-justice system sufficient to assure "fundamental fairness." The process was to be conceived as adversarial—youngsters were held to have rights to counsel, notice of charges, confrontation of witnesses, and acquittal, save upon proof beyond a reasonable doubt of guilt. In the 1970s many states rewrote their juvenile acts to come into compliance with the Supreme Court's constitutional interpretations. Recently federal legislation has been enacted to accelerate the reform process by withholding federal funds from state programs that do not conform to mandated standards. A policy decision seems to have been made at many levels of government to recast the administration of juvenile justice.

But can the new policy be implemented? If one may generalize from the national experience with desegregation, it cannot be said that the impact of the Supreme Court is direct and immediate in producing reform. Nevertheless, events have been influenced by the Warren Court's activism. Resistance to reform in the juvenile-justice system could certainly be expected. Over two-thirds of a century the bureaucracy has evolved a modus vivandi; the judges have become accustomed to power and entrenched in their ways. But surely it could be expected that the resistance would falter and yield to the rule of law. However much the juvenile courts may have resented the state and federal legislation and appellate-court decisions restricting their jurisdiction and modifying their procedures, still they could be expected to obey the law.

Of course the law is sometimes vague. Phrases such as "all deliberate speed," "the rule of reason," and "the best interests of the child" invite interpretation and misunderstanding. But when the law is precise and explicit, surely public officials can be expected to obey it. Elected officials may sometimes resist to the utmost for political or ideological reasons, but bureaucrats and judges are expected to implement the edicts of legitimate authority, or else it is a patent sham to claim that we live under the rule of law.

Yet the central finding of this study is widespread noncompliance among juvenile court judges with very specific legislative requirements (for example, alleged delinquents shall not be detained for more than three days without a hearing). The line between discretion and lawlessness has become blurred.

This witty and elegant book examines the blurred line from an organizational and interorganizational perspective. The author leads the reader through several bodies of relevant literature, describes a strange methodological history in straightforward terms, presents the data convincingly, and speculates intelligently about the way in which reforms aimed at reducing discretion ought to be pursued. This book is a contribution not only to the field of juvenile justice but also to the fields of policy analysis and sociological jurisprudence.

Daniel Katkin
Chairperson,
Administration of Justice Program
The Pennsylvania State University

Acknowledgments

I am indebted to Dr. Jerome Miller and Dr. Harvey Lowell for inviting me to participate in the data-collection process which both inspired and provided the data for the present study.

I am also indebted to my wife and my mother for their encouragement, their patience, and their occasional impatience. Without their support this experience—and perhaps this final product—would have suffered.

Discretion and Lawlessness: Compliance in the Juvenile Court

1 Introduction

Recently, progressively more contentious discussion concerning such issues as governmental accountability, responsiveness, competence, discretion, lawlessness, and compliance has been heard. It would be naive to suggest that misgivings and apprehensions about the proper role and power of government are uniquely contemporary phenomena. A casual reading of the United States Constitution and the Bill of Rights confirms that the Founding Fathers were more than modestly distrustful of a centralized, national government. The primary message of conservative social philosophy from that period to the present has been to warn against the dangers of excessive governmental intervention and power.

Both liberals and conservatives (and the putatively more neutral descriptions of social scientists) have a view of government that is dysfunctionally formal, literal, and legalistic. Legislation and court decisions are discussed as though their expectations were inherently self-initiating and self-limiting.

No one is inclined to think of the criminal or civil law governing the behavior of individuals as self-initiating. The criminal or civil law without enforcement mechanisms and sanctioning power is virtually unthinkable. Both criminal and civil law assumes noncompliance and proceeds on that assumption. Much law, however, speaks to the behavior of government. And with respect to government, the conventional assumption is that government does as the law instructs. The "legal realistics" of the 1920s and 1930s were an exception. Their concerns, however, focused almost exclusively on court behavior, and their impact has been confined to the rather narrow sphere of academic law-school philosophy.

This is not to suggest that Americans have been oblivious to official corruption, scandal, or governmental inefficiency. These terms suggest, however, that such failures are attributable to either individual deviance motivated by personal gain or deviance occasioned by personal incompetence. Even where corruption is seen as pervasive, the language employed to discuss the phenomena limits attention to deviation from formal, legal expectations to only those circumstances involving personal gain and abuse of power. Otherwise, discussion of governmental behavior at the aggregate or individual official level is premised on a tacit assumption of correspondence between formal, legalistic, prescriptive expectations and actual behavior. Only recently has extensive attention begun to focus on unanticipated deviations of official action from the formal expectations of law.

Without denying the inherent interest of the question, this book does not seek an exhaustive explanation of factors underlying this contemporary shift of attention. The widespread popularity of this view may be partly attributable to influences such as the civil-rights movement, the unpopular military involvement in Southeast Asia, the Watergate affair, and the alleged deterioration of respect for traditional authority said to characterize contemporary culture. To accept these explanations uncritically, however, might be to fall victim to the casual reasoning of the mass media and popular cultural commentators. These so-called causes may only be evidence that such a critical mentality already existed. This book is less concerned with the manner in which the issue arose than with an examination of its implications and consequences.

It is self-evident that issues regarding official discretion, compliance, accountability, and responsiveness have emerged as contemporary social problems. James F. Davis (1970) has argued convincingly that cultural perception and opinion have as much if not more to do with the definition of social problems than do questions of the incidence, prevalence, or magnitude of the objective behavior or condition under consideration. It is neither trivial nor mundane to suggest that something is a social problem because it is perceived as a social problem.

Governmental self-regulation, discretion, and compliance in the context of juvenile-court response to legislative change are examined. Chapter 2 selectively reviews the history of the juvenile-court movement and focuses exclusively on the status of discretion in the juvenile court. The role of discretionary rhetoric in expanding, justifying, or protecting the prerogatives of the juvenile court is considered. The Supreme Court's decisions in *Kent* (1966), *Gault* (1969), and *Winship* (1969) are the first major formal attacks on the discretionary authority of the court. Studies of compliance with and the impact of *Gault* suggest, however, that these court decisions had little effect on the day-to-day operation of the juvenile courts.

Most states have revised their juvenile-court law since *Gault*. Generally speaking, these revisions have been consistent with the

Supreme Court decisons. Elements of these statutory changes have reinforced the legal effort to restrict the juvenile courts' power. These legislative changes may be considered merely cosmetic or symbolic attempts to create an appearance of propriety and not genuinely intended to restrict the courts' function. Such a view is often based on an assumption that the juvenile court's real function is social control—usually a very class-conscious social control. I am sympathetic to such a view; however, it is still necessary to differentiate between legislative and judicial action which is allegedly symbolic and that action which must, at least occasionally, be intended in good faith. How is the public official informed as to whether a particular legislative or judicial expectation is seriously intended or whether its purpose is merely to symbolically reassure some momentarily discontented segment of the population? This type of analysis would still require an examination of the specific dynamics of compliance, of the day-to-day organizational environmental consequences of compliance and noncompliance.

In chapter 2 the specific provisions of the Pennsylvania Juvenile Court Act (1973) are examined. Although these provisions anticipate no dramatic or revolutionary change in court behavior, they are unique in juvenile-court legislation because of the specificity and clarity of their expectations. Certain practices are required within specific time periods, that is, detention hearings within seventy-two hours or specific practices or possible outcomes are prohibited. The language of the legislation is sufficiently precise and unambiguous so that although circumvention is possible, overt noncompliance is unlikely.

Chapter 2 also considers several recent amendments to the Pennsylvania Juvenile Court Act. Recent federal legislation relative to juvenile justice is reviewed. The potential impact of the legislation on the court's discretionary power is considered, as is the likelihood of court compliance. The consequences of the new Juvenile Court Act, it is subsequent amendments, and the federal legislation have made previously legal discretionary options illegal. Stated another way, noncompliance is a necessary court response if it is to preserve its previous discretionary prerogatives.

This book discusses that the government's ability to control its own behavior is currently a social problem, official "abuse" of discretion is a social problem, and official compliance and noncompliance is a social problem. Chapter 3 reviews the literature on discretion and compliance. The literature on discretion documents the extent to which extralegal (often socially and ethically questionable) criteria influence official decision making. The literature on compliance demonstrates that neither statutory requirements nor court decisions are necessarily sufficient to ensure that official actors will do as instructed. This observation appears to hold equally for prescriptive and prohibitory expectations. Researchers have so consistently selected situations in which discretion is both so extensive and problematic or in which noncompliance is so pervasive that one might be inclined to conclude that discretion is always abused and noncompliance is universal.

Simultaneously one is faced with a public and social-scientific view of public bureaucracy that has frequently observed or lamented the ritualistic overcompliance of officials to rules and regulations. Thus a major problem for organizations is to induce employees to accept and exercise discretionary authority (Thompson 1967). Both the arguments and observations regarding bureaucratic overcompliance and the findings of the discretion and compliance literature reviewed in chapter 3 are convincing but apparently contradictory. It is possible that organizational theorists have attended to internally generated expectations, whereas the compliance and discretion literature has dealt with externally generated expectations. Varying degrees of official responsiveness to these different sources of authority can be hypothesized. A more interesting and daring line of speculation suggests that officials in organizations in which outcome measures were (or were believed to be) objectively measurable and where officials were held accountable for differential outcomes might seek to avoid discretionary authority. Where outcomes either cannot be or are not believed to be measurable, the exercise of discretion may be attractive. Obviously these differences can exist not only between organizations but between different units of the same organization and even between different role requirements of the same office. Despite this alternate and contradictory view of bureaucratic responsiveness to formal rules and expectations, it is clear that current literature on discretion and compliance is limited to instances involving substantial discretion and noncompliance.

Because social scientists have constantly chosen to examine discretion and compliance in situations where it was known to be problematic, there is little comparable knowledge about factors associated with compliance or about discretionary authority in routine, noncontentious situations. Consequently the compliance literature is about noncompliance rather than compliance; much is known about uncontrolled discretion but little about effectively controlled discretion.

Another problem discussed more extensively in chapter 3 is that the discretion literature seeks to explain differences in decisional outcomes as consequences of either the individual characteristics of clients or decision makers. This research is socially and politically significant because it has focused on the relationship between variables such as age, sex, race, class, and demeanor and discretionary decision making. While the assumption that these variables are the cause of differential decision making is open to question, there is little question that the consequence of this decision making is that the poor, the lower class, racial and ethnic minorities, women, the very young and very old are disproportionately assigned to the least preferred outcomes. The strength of the literature is as a contribution to identification of social problems. An almost identical argument can and should be made with regard to the compliance literature. But because of this focus on individual characteristics, the literature is not particularly instructive for efforts that seek to understand the dynamics of discretion or compliance nor for efforts to understand how discretion might be controlled or compliance achieved.

Reducing official discretion or increased levels of official compliance is not advocated. It is necessary to differentiate between an analytical interest in those conditions that lead to reduced discretion and increased compliance, and an essentially political position that demands a reduction in discretion and an increase in compliance. The ideology of most of the researchers currently writing on discretion and compliance is liberal. The compliance literature exclusively examines noncompliance with liberal legislation and court decisions. Liberals were historically the principal defenders of official discretion because they once believed it was more conducive to the advancement of their ideological interest. They have currently been proven wrong in this assumption. Just as the liberal mentality learned that its approval of discretion was at best situational, it is even more clear that one's appreciation of compliance or disapproval of noncompliance is contingent on the specifics of the particular statute or court decision in question. Those whose personal ideological position leads them currently to lament the noncompliance of public officials may come to applaud noncompliance in the face of other, more personally distasteful legislative or court action.

Chapter 3 seeks to clarify definitions of discretion and compliance. It demonstrates the inadequacies of these literatures and shows that there is a considerably greater interrelationship between discretion and compliance than has been previously noted. A recommendation is made for a diminution of attention to personal and demographic characteristics in the study of discretion and compliance to be replaced by attention to organizational and environmental inducements and constraints.

Chapter 4 describes a study of nonurban Pennsylvania juvenile-court detention practices in 1975—two years after passage of the new Juvenile Court Act. This study was conducted under the auspices of the Pennsylvania Department of Public Welfare. Despite the department's clear statutory authority in this area, much of the data had to be pursued indirectly in deference to the courts' ability to deny access. Even with the modest and noncontentious survey instrument that was formally adopted, researchers were forbidden access to several of the selected counties, prohibited from personally seeing court files in several others, and had their data confiscated by the juvenile-court judge in one county. (Chapter 5 argues that the juvenile court's ability to operate in secrecy, control and manipulate all relevant data about its operations, and frustrate and even forbid other agencies, such as the Department of Public Welfare, from performing legislatively mandated oversight functions is centrally related to the court's ability to avoid compliance and ignore court and legislative efforts to control or regulate its power.) Because of differential access to official court records, substantial differences in record-keeping practices in the various counties, and because the researchers were dependent on the voluntary cooperation of juvenile-court personnel, it would be both naive and unconvincing to pretend that the data collected was sufficiently precise to justify elaborated statistical comparisons. The formal survey data together with observational data compiled covertly during the course of the study are sufficient to assert the following:

1. All current statistical data provided by the individual juvenile courts, through traditional reporting mechanisms within the Department of Public Welfare and by the Juvenile Court Judges Commission, are grossly inaccruate even with regard to such apparently unproblematic issues as number of juveniles detained, length of detention, and reason for detention.

2. Noncompliance is so pervasive that it is not even possible to

compare high-compliance and low-compliance counties as was originally intended. Even where some modest movement toward compliance may be noted with respect to a particular expectation, factors other than those traditionally associated with compliance are more appropriate explanations of such phenomena.

3. Even though this research focused on the impact of recent state legislation rather than on the earlier Supreme Court decisions, no evidence was uncovered that suggests that the Supreme Court decisions have had any impact on the operational reality or on the decisional alternatives available to the court. This is not to suggest that the juvenile court may not be any different now than it was prior to the mid-1960s nor that the Supreme Court decisions may not have indirectly contributed to such difference as might exist. However, none of the formal expectations of *Gault*, were observable in the nonurban Pennsylvania juvenile courts studied in 1975.

Had high- and low-compliance counties been identifiable, had the researchers been permitted to directly and systematically examine the issues of interest to them, and had juvenile-court records been sufficient to supply the required data, this book might have resembled many of the compliance discretion studies reviewed in chapter 3. If high- and low-compliance counties had emerged, these variables would have been examined with regard to some of the following dimensions: tenure of the judge on the juvenile-court bench; political affiliation of the judge and the county government currently in power; the judge's involvement (high or low) in the activities of the state Juvenile Court Judges Commission; age, sex, racial, and class characteristics of the offending population. Although discretion studies have partially explained differences in outcome as a consequence of factors such as those suggested above, compliance studies have been unsuccessful in such attempts. Stapleton and Teitlebaum (1973) conclude that juvenile-court compliance with Supreme Court decisions is relatively high in jurisdictions in which judges are new to the bench and relatively low where judges' tenure is longer. Were the purpose of this book confined to an attempt to confirm the Stapleton and Teitlebaum hypothesis, it is self-evident that their hypothesis could not survive a Pennsylvania test. Pennsylvania judges differ markedly in terms of the length of their service on the juvenile-court bench, yet there was no difference in rates of compliance.

By applying identical logic, hypotheses suggesting that any difference among the counties studied has an impact on compliance can be refuted. The single exception to this uniform pattern of noncompliance is Philadelphia County. Interviews suggest that the Philadelphia County Juvenile Court was close to complying with many of the provisions of the Juvenile Court Act in 1975 and has subsequently come into full or near-full compliance. (Data on detention incidents from Philadelphia County, however, were not collected during the formal part of the study as reported in chapter 4). Philadelphia County differs from the counties studied in ways that suggest that noncompliance in Philadelphia would exceed noncompliance in other counties. The opposite is true, and chapter 5 offers several hypotheses to explain the phenomena. The most attractive explanation is the historically aggressive role of defense counsel, which is generally provided through public funds in the Philadelphia court.

In much the same manner of earlier compliance studies, chapter 4 establishes the pervasiveness of noncompliance. Chapter 5, however, explains noncompliance in a way that breaks substantially with the traditional compliance literature. The data reported in chapter 4 establish the fact that the juvenile courts, whose detention practices were studied, ignored the expectations established in the new Juvenile Court Act. Chapter 5 identifies organizational and environmental factors that explain the court's ability to successfully avoid compliance and specifies the additional conditions necessary to obtain compliance. It examines the theoretical and prescriptive utility of the following assumptions:

1. The presence of regulatory, enforcement, compliance, and oversight mechanisms and strategies is essential to the achievement of reduced discretion and compliance. In the absence of these mechanisms and strategies, legislation that seeks to regulate and control governmental action becomes functionally nothing more than enabling legislation.

2. Client resources are relevant to the control of discretion and the achievement of compliance. Davis (1969) and Jowell (1975) provide support for the contention that discretion is limited and compliance with formally generated expectations is achieved in situations in which subjects of official decision making have sufficient status and resources. Clearly the clients of the juvenile court possess as limited an array of resources as any imaginable group. To the extent that enforcement responsibilities reside—by default—with the subjects of official action, compliance and limitations on discretion are not to be

anticipated except where such self-restraint serves some other individual or organizational function.

3. Perhaps the most significant obstacle to compliance in the juvenile court is the court's functional dominance of all organizations within their sphere of interest. The Juvenile Court Judges Commission has acquired responsibility for most monitoring, reporting, and policy functions relevant to the juvenile court. The Department of Public Welfare, which possesses both direct and indirect statutory authority with respect to key elements of juvenile justice, has historically behaved as if its sole purpose was to serve the convenience of the court. Pennsylvania appellate courts have consistently maintained a policy of nonintervention in juvenile court matters. Any one of these three sources had sufficient resources and authority to demand at least technical compliance of the court, none did.

4. Critics of the juvenile court have frequently noted the effect that social-work rhetoric has on distorting and concealing the more coercive and punitive elements of court practice. In more universal terms, Edelman (1977) examines the role of "symbolic language" in concealing, justifying, and otherwise obscuring the nature and function of government action. The manner in which social-work techniques protect the court from oversight or review is less obvious. The United States Supreme Court was forced to reconstruct the proceedings of the juvenile court in *Gault* from testimony in the Arizona Supreme Court habeas corpus hearing because no transcript of the original proceedings existed. Pennsylvania researchers searched page after page of juvenile-court case files in an attempt to locate delinquency petitions, reasons for detention, and even confirmation that a child had been detained. On several occasions I read one- to three-page entries in a case file dated during the period when a child was in detention but which contained no reference to the detention incident. No matter how benign the intent of juvenile-court record-keeping practices, no finer strategy could be conceived to protect the court from external review. When one adds to this the court's incessant cant of "confidentiality," the court becomes virtually impervious to external restraints. It can be argued that "confidentiality" represents a greater boon to the interests of the court than the interests of the juvenile.

It is possible that two years is too short a period to say anything conclusive about compliance. It may be argued that reform of this sort is evolutionary and what should be considered are the processes by which innovation becomes implemented and regularized over time. Obviously, the comparison of 1975 statistics with those from subsequent years could be enlightening. The reader is reminded, however, how bizarre such a conception of compliance would be were it applied to criminal or civil law. Can one imagine the IRS waiting patiently for years until taxpayers were inclined to adapt to changes in the tax laws? The credibility of the above perspective is another instance of the peculiar assumptions held about the relationship between law and government.

Concepts such as discretion, compliance, accountability, government responsiveness, administrative rule making, regulatory administration, and government lawlessness have more in common than has been previously acknowledged. Were compliance and discretion studied with respect to less contentious and highly charged ideological issues, more useful general hypotheses might be generated. It is possible to compare high-compliance with low-compliance situations and controlled-discretion with uncontrolled-discretion situations only when more is known about compliance and controlled discretion. The more prescriptive aspirations of proposals for administrative rule making, regulatory administration, and other efforts to ensure governmental responsiveness and accountability are only likely to produce results if they are guided by knowledge about the dynamics of discretion and compliance.

Chapter 6 also considers the need for additional definitional clarity of the terms discretion, compliance, accountability, and regulation. It may be fruitful to examine discretion and compliance in a manner analogous to deterrence studies in criminal justice. Further study of the role, function, and utility of rules in public organizations would be helpful. Finally, several additional issues relative to the study of discretion and compliance are speculatively considered.

2 Discretion and the Juvenile Court

Although the juvenile court's formal history began with the passage in 1899 of the first juvenile-court act in Illinois, the first institution for children convicted of criminal offenses, the New York City House of Refuge, was created in 1824. By the time the first juvenile-court act took effect there were sixty-five institutions for children in the United States. The avowed purpose of the juvenile-court reformers, according to most histories of juvenile justice, was to put an end to the brutal, harsh, and essentially nonrehabilitative treatment children received at the hands of the adult court. From its inception, the juvenile court alleged to be founded on a social-work rather than a criminal-court model. As such, its avowed concern was with the "best interests of the child," protecting the child, and assisting the child on the path to "good, sound, adult citizenship." To this end the court adopted the common-law doctrine of parens patriae, which holds that the state as ultimate parent has responsibility and power over minors (and others unable to care for themselves). While a careful historical inquiry into parens patriae practice in English common law indicates that the crown invoked this state power most frequently as a means of obtaining control of the estates of wealthy orphans, it is generally assumed that the intentions of juvenile-court reformers were more benign.

However much the doctrine of parens patriae may have been an invention of convenience, it served the juvenile court well in establishing and expanding its jurisdiction. The earliest juvenile codes confined the jurisdiction of the juvenile court to youthful law violation, however, the scope of the court's domain was quickly expanded to include numerous noncriminal behaviors. By 1907 in Illinois "delinquent" was defined by the state's juvenile code as follows:

> The words "delinquent child" shall mean any male child who while under the age of seventeen years or any female child who while under the age of eighteen years violates any law of the State; or is incorrigible, or knowingly associates with thieves, vicious or immoral persons; or without just cause

> and without consent of its parents, guardian or custodian absents itself from its home or place of abode, or is growing up in idleness or crime, or knowingly frequents a house of ill-repute; or knowingly frequents any policy shop or place where any gaming device is operated; or frequents any saloon or dram shop where intoxicating liquors are sold; or patronizes or visits any pool room or bucket shop; or wanders the streets in the night time without being on (any) lawful business or lawful occupation; or habitually wanders about any railroad yard or tracks or attempts to jump on any car or engine without lawful authority; or uses vile, obscene, vulgar, profane or indecent language in (any) public place or about any school house; or is guilty of indecent or lascivious conduct; any child committing any of these acts herein shall be deemed a delinquent child.

Many juvenile courts accepted their authority as parent quite literally; at least the parental model was used extensively to justify jurisdiction and court practices. Courts insisted that they be judged not by standards of appropriate state intervention in the affairs of individual citizens but relative to what one might reasonably expect of a father's behavior toward a wayward child. In *Commonwealth* v. *Fisher* (1905) the Pennsylvania Supreme Court held:

> The natural parent needs no (due) process to temporarily deprive his child of liberty by confining it in its own home, to save it and to shield it from the consequences of persistence in a career of waywardness, nor is the state, when compelled as parens patriae, to take the place of the father for the same purpose required to adopt any (due) process as a means of placing its hands upon the child to lead it into one of its courts.

In the same spirit, Judge Ben Lindsey of the Denver Juvenile Court observed (Lindsey 1904):

> [W]e pay very little attention to rules of evidence. . . . The whole proceedings is in the interest of the child and not to degrade him or even to punish him. We do not protect the child by discharging him because there is no legal evidence to convict, as would be done in a criminal case when we know that he has committed the offense. This is to do him a great injury, for he is simply encouraged in the prevalent opinion among city children . . . that it is all right to lie all you can, to cheat all you can, to steal all you can, so long as they "do not get caught" or that you have "no proof."

Implicit in the role of parent was the appropriateness of preventative intervention. Unlike the adult system of criminal justice, the juvenile court did not feel obliged to await criminal misconduct before intervening. The juvenile court was alleged to have the right (many called it duty) to intervene with the child who was in danger of becoming delinquent. Thus the effective jurisdiction of the juvenile court was limited only by the court's imagination regarding the types of situations in which its services might prove useful.

Since the juvenile court was conceptualized as a civil rather than a criminal proceeding, its motive for intervention was alleged to be helpful rather than punitive, and helpful intervention was thought to demand the full cooperation of the client, juvenile courts excused themselves from the procedural and substantive requirements associated with criminal law. In juvenile court informality was not defended as an expediency; it was embraced as a necessary and inherently desirable element of the process. Broad discretionary powers were not excused but were glorified as the vehicle through which the rehabilitative goals of the system would be realized.

Little purpose is served by questioning the sincerity of the intentions of juvenile-court reformers. It might be argued that sanctions against youthful offenders in cases involving misdemeanors and minor criminal violations were probably increasingly difficult to obtain in adult court (particularly if the minor opted for a jury trial), and the parens patriae model of juvenile justice was merely a device to control and regulate the behavior of youth (particularly the urban lower classes). But to suggest that these were the motives that underlay the creation of the juvenile court would be to do disservice to history as history. It must be observed, however, that even though no one involved in the creation of the court may have envisioned or intended it, procedural informality, discretionary authority, and extreme enthusiasm in the pursuit of well-intentioned goals led to practices that later observers have viewed with considerable alarm. The spirit in which the juvenile court was received is articulately stated by Hutchins (1976, p. vii, viii).

> When I graduated from law school some fifty years ago, the aspiring liberals among us thought we knew what was the trouble with the law. It was too narrow and too formalistic . . . we hailed those developments which emphasized the differences in "fact situations," which required the interposition of the social sciences, and which sought to temper the wind to the shorn lamb by the exercise of discretion. . . . The juvenile court, then only twenty-five years old, reflected the state as parens patriae, which could rescue children from the law, and from those agents of government whom we did not trust, like policemen, prosecutors, judges in criminal courts, and wardens of jails and penitentiaries. To us the juvenile court, with which few of us had any experience, looked like the fulfillment of our dreams. It had come into existence through the efforts of persons whose ideals we shared. It was packed with discretion from stem to stern. It relied on social workers. It aimed at "saving the child," not punishing him. If it

> had not existed, we would have tried to invent it. This calm, judicious, comprehensive book shows how wrong we were.

While men have always been wary of excessive punishment and brutality, the danger of excesses in the provision of help, assistance, and treatment are less easily detected. And it would be a grave error to conclude that the enthusiasm and the potential overzealousness of the early juvenile-court reformers died quickly. Conversations with many juvenile-court probation officers and judges reveal disappointment and disbelief that people of good intention would attempt to prevent them from providing assistance to a troubled child. Although belief may die hard within the profession, the past several decades have produced progressively more urgent appeals to reform juvenile-court procedures, limit court jurisdiction, and eliminate the juvenile court itself.

As early as 1937 Dean Roscoe Pound (1937, p. xxvii) referred to the juvenile court as a "tribunal more awesome in its abuse of power than the Star Chamber," however, widespread criticism of the juvenile court was not heard until the middle of the century. Before long even someone as central to the juvenile-justice profession as Milton Luger, head of the delinquency division of the Law Enforcement Assistance Administration and formerly director of Juvenile Corrections for New York State and chairman of the National Association of State Juvenile Delinquency Program Administrators, was quoted as saying (James 1970): "With the exception of a relatively few youths it (would be) better for all concerned if young delinquents were not detected, apprehended, or institutionalized. Too many of them get worse in our care."

In 1966 the first of four Supreme Court cases involving the conduct of the juvenile court was heard. In *Kent* v. *United States* (383 U.S. 541, 1966) the court observed: "There is evidence, in fact, that there be grounds for concern that the child receives the worst of both worlds: That he gets neither the protections afforded adults nor the solicitous care and regenerative treatment postulated for children." *Kent* was not technically a constitutional case because it was resolved on interpretation of a District of Columbia statute, however, the court's language left little doubt that were a case brought on broader constitutional ground, it would be receptive. In *Kent* the court affirmed the following rights in decisions to waive to adult jurisdiction: a hearing on the waiver decision, the right to counsel, the attorney must be afforded access to the records and reports that are considered in reaching a decision, and the judge must offer a written decision for waiver. In reaching this decision, the court observed that "there is no place in our system of law for reaching a result of such tremendous consequences without ceremony—without hearing, without effective assistance of counsel, without a statement of reason."

In 1967 the Supreme Court made the constitutional character of its decision clear in *In re Gault* (387 U.S. 1, 1967). Extending the principle that the Fourteenth Amendment incorporated the first ten amendments and made them applicable to the states to specific areas of the juvenile court, *Gault* promised the juvenile the following "essentials of due process and fair treatments" when institutionalization might result: the right to notice of charges, the right to counsel, the right to confrontation and cross-examination of witness, and the right to refrain from self-incrimination. In uncharacteristically blunt language Justice Fortas wrote that "under our Constitution, the condition of being a boy does not justify a kangaroo court." In addition, the court expressed its reservations regarding the allegedly nonpunitive character of the juvenile court intervention:

> However euphemistic the title, a "receiving home" or an "industrial school" for juveniles is an institution of confinement in which the child is incarcerated for a greater or lesser time. His world becomes "a building with whitewashed walls, regimented routine and institutional laws." . . . Instead of mother and father and sister and brother and friends and classmates, his world is peopled by guards, custodians, state employees, and "delinquents" confined with him for anything from waywardness to rape and homicide.

In the Supreme Court decision in *In re Winship* (397 U.S. 358, 1970) the requirement of proof "beyond a reasonable doubt" was extended to juvenile-court proceedings alleging delinquency. The court, however, carefully noted that its decision pertained only to delinquency proceedings: "we intimate no view concerning the constitutionality of the New York procedures governing children in need of supervision."

In 1970 in *McKeiver* v. *Pennsylvania* (403 U.S. 528, 1971) at least a temporary end was brought to the extension of full privileges of the adult criminal court to the juvenile justice system. In refusing to extend the right to jury trial to juveniles, the court engaged in this confusing discussion:

> Concern about the inapplicability of exclusionary and other rules of evidence; about the juvenile court judges' possible awareness of the

> juvenile's prior record and of the contents of the social file; about repeated appearances of the same familiar witnesses in the persons of juvenile and probation officers and social workers—all to the effect that this will create the likelihood of pre-judgement—chooses to ignore, it seems to us, every aspect of fairness, of concern, of sympathy, and of paternal attention that the juvenile court system contemplates.
>
> If the formalities of the criminal adjudicative process are to be superimposed upon the juvenile court system, there is little need for its separate existence. Perhaps that ultimate disillusionment will come one day, but for the moment we are disinclined to give impetus to it.

With these words the court entered perhaps the strangest defense of juvenile court practice on record.

After this series of Supreme court decisions, lower courts, which had previously been reluctant to intervene in the juvenile-court arena, refined and expanded the higher court's position. Numerous federal and state courts have held that juvenile pretrial detention requires a prompt determination of probable cause as a matter of federal constitutional law: *Cooley* v. *Stone*, 414 F. 2d 1213 (D.C. Cir. 1969); *Moss* v. *Weaver*, 383 F. Supp. 130 (1974), aff'd in part, rev'd in part, 525 F. 2d 1258 (5th Cir. 1976); *In re a juvenile*, 306 N.E. 2d 822 (Mass. 1974). While most courts have held that juveniles have no right to bail: *Baker* v. *Smith*, 477 S.W. 2d 149 (Ky, 1972); *R.* v. *Whitmer*, 515 P. 2d 617 (Utah 1973), 62 N.E. 2d 268 (Ohio, 1945); *A.N.E.* v. *State*, 156 So. 2d 525 (Fla. App. 1963), at least two have ruled that bail is constitutionally required: *Trimble* v. *Stone*, 187 F. Supp. 483 (D.C. 1960); *State* v. *Hundley*, 267 So. 2d 207 (La. 1972). Several state courts including Pennsylvania's have decided that continued detention requires substantial evidence that such detention is necessary: *In re Macidon*, 49 Cal. Rptr. 861, (Cal. App. 1966); *Commonwealth ex rel. Sprowal* v. *Hendricks* 265 A. 2d 348 (PA. 1970). Courts have frequently ruled in favor of juveniles in cases involving care and treatment in detention: *Martarella* v. *Kelley*, 349 F. Supp. 575 (S.D.N.Y. 1972); *Creek* v. *Stone*, 379 F. 2d 106 (D.C. Cir. 1967); *Baker* v. *Hamilton*, 345 F. Supp. 345 (W.D. Ky. 1972); *Swansey* v. *Elrod*, 386 F. Supp. 1138 (N.D. Ill, 1975); *Manney* v. *Cabell*, No. 75-3305-R (C.D. Cal. 1976); *Tommy P.* v. *Spokane School District*, No. 224974 (Wash. Super. Ct., Spokane Cty. 1976); *Roe* v. *Commonwealth of Pa.*, Civ Action No. 74-519 (W.D. Pa. 1976).

Despite some confusion, the court decision in this series of cases led many observers to conclude that the form and character of the juvenile court would be dramatically changed. It was assumed that the right to counsel and other trappings of the adversarial model would make the model of practice in the juvenile court very similar to that of the adult criminal court. Several studies of the impact of *Gault*, however, sounded a more cautionary note. Lefstein, Stapleton, and Teitlebaum (1969) report on an observational study of cases involving unrepresented juveniles in three metropolitan courts. Extensive compliance was observed in one city, but compliance was minimal in the other two. With reference to the right to counsel, the authors note "full advice," "partial advice," and "no advice." In the two low-compliance cities 0 percent and 3 percent of the juveniles were fully advised of their rights, 15 percent and 65 percent were partially advised, and 85 percent and 32 percent were not advised at all. In one city the right against self-incrimination was never mentioned; in the other it was mentioned in only 29 percent of the cases. Even this may overstate the case for compliance since the authors observe that even when juveniles were informed or partially informed, it was often done in a manner thought likely to discourage the exercise of those rights. In the one high-compliance court, judges were new to the bench, whereas judges in the low-compliance courts had extensive juvenile-court experience. The authors attribute the dramatic differences in rates of compliance to this factor.

In a follow-up study of dispositional consequences, Stapleton and Teitlebaum (1973) compare outcomes of juveniles represented and unrepresented by counsel in the high-compliance city and one of the low-compliance cities previously studied. Although methodological problems make exact comparisons difficult, it is apparent from the data that representation by counsel in the high-compliance city resulted in slightly higher dismissal rates and slightly lower commitment rates. In the low-compliance city dismissal rates for represented and unrepresented juveniles were similar, but commitment rates were higher for juveniles represented by counsel than for those not represented. This latter finding holds even when the authors attempt to control for potential differences in severity of offense(s) between represented and unrepresented juveniles.

In a study of compliance with *Gault* in rural Kentucky Canon and Kolson (1971) observe that the juvenile's decision to be represented by counsel is "the kiss of death." Other lawyers and juvenile-court commentators have suggested that representation of counsel, particularly aggressive, adversarial representation, in some jurisdictions and with some judges, produces dispositional outcomes inconsistent with the client's interest. If representation by counsel prejudices the defendant's case in situations where the court disapproves of such representation and in the absence of remedy for such bias, the right to counsel must be seen as a hollow victory.

In response to *Gault* and the growing criticism of the juvenile justice system as an excessively discretionary system, most states revised or amended their juvenile-court acts. On 6 December 1972 the governor of Pennsylvania signed a new juvenile-court act (act 333 of 1972). Although the new act and the provisions of the 1933 act are similar, the new act specifically extends the right to counsel in all hearings, introduces a requirement for mandatory hearings, and imposes several limits on detention practices. The following requirements are particularly interesting:

1. Detained juveniles must receive a detention hearing within seventy-two hours (section 15, b).
2. A child detained (when permissible under the act) in a jail or other facility with adults may be held "under such circumstances for not more than five days" (section 14, a, 4).
3. A child detained (in any permissible circumstance) must receive an adjudicatory hearing within ten days (section 18, a).
4. A child alleged to be deprived "shall not be detained in a jail or other facility intended or used for the detention of adults charged with criminal offenses or of children alleged to be delinquent" (section 14, d).
5. Detention center or shelter-care facilities must be used to detain juveniles rather than jail when such facilities are available; that is, the use of jails to detain juveniles is only permitted when "there is no other appropriate facility available" (section 14, a, 4).
6. All commitments initiated under the act must be reviewed every six months and "dispositional review hearings" must be held at least every twelve months (section 26).

In most respects the hearing requirements are similar to the requirements imposed in *Kent, Gault*, and *Winship* in that they require procedural changes that may alter the outcome at various decisional points. Although hearings are required and rights to counsel at all hearings are extended, the legislation does not speak to the substance of such hearings. For instance, it is possible that ritualistic hearings would arrive at the same outcome as would have been obtained before hearings were mandated. The requirements imposed on detention practices are perhaps more forceful because they absolutely prohibit certain decisional outcomes.

The clarity and precision of the language of the legislation makes the six requirements listed previously potentially forceful. There are no phrases such as all deliberate speed, timely determination, least restrictive alternative, essentials of due process and fair treatment, or maximum feasible participation. Conspicuously absent are words and phrases which, while expedient for achieving consensus in multimember courts and legislative bodies, are likely to lead to confusion, conflicting interpretation, and the need for further judicial clarification. Courts might argue that the ten-day adjudicatory hearing required for detained juveniles means ten court working days rather than ten calendar days (the juvenile-court legislation in numerous other states, for example, states such requirements in terms of court working days). It is possible to argue, by perverting the obvious logic of the statute and taking the phrase completely out of context, that detention centers or shelter-care facilities are not "appropriate facilities" for certain juveniles, and therefore the legislation does not prohibit use of county jails when detention centers exist. Even here these two potential sources of conflicting interpretation are subject to easy resolution.

It would be frivolous to suggest that the Pennsylvania Juvenile Court Act sought to radically overhaul juvenile-court practice, as some claimed the *Gault* decision intended. Unlike the decision in *Gault*, however, the statute does not purport to assure "fundamental fairness." For most areas of court decision making, the legislation left the discretionary authority of the court untouched. It speaks of an expectation of detention centers and shelter-care facilities rather than jail for juvenile detention, but it provides the court the opportunity to use jails for detention in the absence of appropriate facilities. With reference to the six requirements listed previously, however, the statute is specific and its meaning is unequivocal. Thus areas of decision making that had once been within the realm of the court's discretionary authority are illegal.

In 1976 the Juvenile Court Act of 1972 was amended, changing the pattern of state reimbursement to counties for juvenile services (Public Law 148, 1976). Previous to this amendment, state policy, contrary to the protestations of Department of Public Welfare officials and members of the governor's staff, favored institutional placement of youthful offenders over community placement. The state, prior to the 1976 amendment, reimbursed the counties for 100 percent of the costs for maintenance of youths in state facilities and 50 percent of the costs for private facilities . Counties were reimbursed for only 50 percent of the costs associated with community programs, however. Funding patterns set out in the 1972 statute financially rewarded county courts for opting for institutional placements in state-run facilities. The amendment changed the reimbursement formula to 50 percent reimbursement to counties for all state and private institutional costs and raised the reimbursement for community-based services to 75 to 90 percent. Even though the Department of Public Welfare confused the issue by designating numerous state and private institutions as community-based facilities, the 1976 legislation can be viewed as an attempt by the legislature to encourage a reduction in the number of juveniles committed to institutions.

In 1977 the legislature undertook a significantly more aggressive attempt to reshape juvenile-court practice. Public Law 41 (1977) contained the following provisions:

1. The definition of "delinquent act" was amended to omit reference to status offenses (section 2, 2). "Deprived child" was changed to "dependent child," and status offenses were reintroduced under this classification (section 2, 4).

2. The amendment deleted the language permitting the use of jails for detention ("unless there is no appropriate facility available"), in which case section 14, 4 as amended read: "Under no circumstances shall a child be detained, placed, or committed in any facility with adults, or where he or she is apt to be abused by other children." Counties were given until 31 December 1979 to comply.

3. In the interim jails could be used to detain juveniles only if: "such detention is necessary for the safety of the public," the jail was approved by the Department of Public Welfare for the detention of juveniles, and "such detention is ordered by the court" (section 14, 4, b, 1).

4. Counties were required to submit a plan for removal of all juveniles from adult facilities by 31 December 1978. If such a plan was not received, the Department of Public Welfare was instructed to "take what steps it deems necessary to provide the required detention services for any such counties; including the construction of a regional detention facility." If state or federal funds were not available for this purpose, the Department of Public Welfare "shall charge the

cost of establishing the necessary regional detention facilities to the counties'' up to $50,000 (section 14, 4, f, 1). This is the first instance in which Pennsylvania juvenile-court law anticipates noncompliance and specifies a remedy for such noncompliance as may occur. Previous statutory language tacitly presupposed compliance since the consequences of noncompliance were never attended to.

5. A child alleged to be dependent (which now included all status offenders) could be detained or placed only in a Department of Public Welfare approved shelter-care facility. The development of shelter-care facilities were mandated (section 14, 4, d and e).

6. The requirement that ''probable cause'' be established in detention hearings of juveniles alleged to be delinquent was added to preexisting language.

7. If a child was detained a petition had to be filed with the court ''within twenty-four hours or the next court business day of the child's admission to detention or shelter care.'' The old language read that the petition ''shall be promptly made'' (section 15, a).

8. The court was instructed to ''impose the minimum amount of confinement that is consistent with the protection of the public and the rehabilitative needs of the child'' (section 25, 4).

9. Institutions were given the authority to institute transfers of youths to less secure facilities ''including a group home or a foster boarding home.'' The institutions were required to give the committing court written notice of such intentions. The court had ten days to object to such transfer, otherwise the institution could proceed on its own authority (section 26, b). Previous to this provision the court had full control of commitment, transfer, and release decisions.

10. The Department of Public Welfare was given the authority to ''temporarily close'' an institution that was 110 percent of its stated capacity to further court referrals (section 26, c). Previously institutions were compelled to accept all juvenile court referrals, regardless of their population, under threat of contempt proceedings.

Only the requirements of the 1972 Juvenile Court Act were applicable restrictions on court practice during 1975. Pennsylvania Public Laws 148 of 1976 and 41 of 1977 were not binding on the court during the period of time studied. These two pieces of legislation, however, lend considerable support to the argument that concern about the appropriateness of juvenile-court functioning was widespread and efforts were seriously being undertaken to delimit the court's authority and power. More significantly, this legislation plus the Federal Juvenile Justice and Delinquency Prevention Act (1974) ultimately may form the basis of enforcement and regulation relative to juvenile-court practice. It might be argued that the 1972 legislation, which only modestly revised the forty-year-old Juvenile Court Act of 1933, was enacted to give the Pennsylvania juvenile justice system the appearance of respectability with respect to recent court decisions and the clamor for reform. If the 1972 legislation stood alone, this might be a creditable hypothesis. But given the aggressive content of the 1976 and 1977 amendments, it seems that the legislature's intent to bring the juvenile court under tighter control is genuine.

The state of Washington, for instance, has gone much further in its attempts to redefine the authority of the juvenile court. A new law, signed in June 1977 which took effect 1 July 1978, substantially alters the court's authority relative to the sentencing of juveniles. Mandatory restitution and "diversion" into community programs is required for youth designated as "minor offenders"; mandatory institutionalization is required for youth designated as "serious offenders." The juvenile-court judge retains traditional dispositional authority only for offenses that lie between these extremes. As envisioned, "community boards will determine restitution and placement in community programs, the prosecutor will determine the charge to be brought, and predetermined minimum-maximum terms are to be set for specific offenses by the Bureau of Juvenile Rehabilitation" (Krajick 1977). While skepticism regarding the impact of this legislation on disposition of juvenile offenders, institutional populations, and actual time served is warranted pending studies of the manner in which these various agencies define the exercise their new authority, the legislature's intent to divest the juvenile court of some of its traditional authority is clear.

Perhaps the most forceful, although indirect, attack on the juvenile court to date has been the closing of juvenile institutions in Massachusetts. While the deinstitutionalization movement has characterized itself as an attack on custodial institutions, the juvenile court cannot reasonably dissociate itself from the implications of such criticism. This is particularly true in states such as Pennsylvania, in which the court itself has complete authority for determining institutional placement and time served. To the extent that the dispositional alternatives available to the court lose credibility, the court loses credibility. Because of the broad discretionary authority of the court with reference to disposition, the court must assume responsibility for the inadequacies of the dispositional options it chooses to employ. It is clear from *Gault* that it was dissatisfaction with the character of juvenile institutions that motivated the Supreme Court's attention to juvenile-court practice.

Conclusion

The juvenile court came into existence at the turn of the century amid much enthusiasm for the potential of social work and clinical and quasi-clinical rehabilitative intervention. Since the juvenile court's role was conceptualized as (parental) assistance and guidance rather than punishment, or because its punitive role was successfully disguised behind its rehabilitative rhetoric, the juvenile court was granted broad discretionary authority. Legislatures and review courts abdicated their regulatory authority and deferred to the competence of juvenile-court and social-work judgment.

By mid-century, however, considerable skepticism had arisen regarding (a) the ability of the social sciences to generate adequate predictive measures, (b) the ability of social work and clinical interventions to produce therapeutic results, (c) the authenticity of the benignly intentioned goals of juvenile justice and other "treatment" interventions, and (d) the equity and fairness of discretionary decision making. In juvenile justice—as was the case in social welfare, mental health, and police, court, and correctional practice in the adult system—appellate courts began to reevaluate their traditional position relative to official discretion. The Supreme Court, particularly in the *Gault* decision, sought to bring the "essentials of due process and fair treatment" to the juvenile court. Compliance and impact studies suggested that juvenile-court practices remained essentially unchanged. Subsequent legislation at both the national and state levels also sought to further regulate aspects of juvenile-court practice.

In Pennsylvania a new juvenile-court act and two amendments to that act made "illegal," in very specific and apparently incontestable language, a number of practices that were previously "legal" under the courts' discretionary authority. In this instance, although certainly not in all instances, noncompliance and "discretionary power" arise as issues simultaneously.

3 Discretion and Compliance

Webster's Third New International Dictionary defines *discretion* as "power of free decision or choice within certain legal bounds," and "ability to make decisions that represent a responsible choice and for which an understanding of what is lawful, right, or wise may be presupposed." *Black's Law Dictionary* (at 553) provides the following discussion of discretion:

> discretion bounded by the rules and principles of law, and not arbitrary, capricious, or unrestrained. "Judicial discretion" is substantially synonymous with judicial power. Griffin v. State, 12 Ga. App. 615, 77 S.E. 1080, 1083. It is not indulgence of a judicial whim, but the exercise of judicial judgment, based on facts and guided by law, Smith v. Hill, C.C.A., 5 F.2d 188, or the equitable decision of what is just and proper under the circumstances, People v. Pfanschmidt, 262 Ill. 411, 104 N.E. 804, 816, Ann. Cas. 1915A, 1171.

The troublesome element in the definitions cited above is the reliance on prescription rather than description. These definitions either tacitly assume that decision makers will routinely confine their decisions to both the expectations of law and the requirements of justice or leave no name for decision-making prerogatives that fail to meet these lofty expectations. They assume that the expectations of law and requirements of justice are universally compatible, the motives of decision makers are above reproach, and decision makers have sufficient competence—acquired through education, training, or experience, presumably—to make these judgments.

Kenneth Culp Davis (1969, p. 4) suggests that "a public officer has discretion whenever the effective limits of his power leave him free to make a choice among possible courses of action or inaction." The phrase "effective limits" is important because it allows for discrepancy between formally imposed limits and limits that are operational and effective in actual decision-making situations. This discrepancy may be in either one or two directions. The least obvious is in situations where the effective limits are more confining than are the formal limits. This is the case with prosecutorial discretion in the

United States. Formally there exist relatively few limits on prosecutorial discretion in either misdemeanor, minor criminal, or major criminal cases. Davis frequently points to the prosecutor's office for examples of extensive discretion. However, in these discussions he fails to attend to the issue of effective limits (Davis 1969, 1976). While it is clear that the prosecutor's discretion is substantially greater in practice in misdemeanor offenses than in major criminal offenses, nothing having to do with formal limits explains this difference. The effective limits of the prosecutor's discretion in major criminal cases must be informal rather than formal; they must be a consequence of environmental rather than legal constraints. The second—and most frequently noted—discrepancy between formal and effective limits on discretion is in situations in which the effective limits go beyond what is permitted or expected by the formal limits. Selective enforcement practices by police are an example of this form of discrepancy. Although every jurisdiction has statutes requiring full enforcement of all laws, every police department engages in selective rather than full enforcement. Here again, since the effective limits are not the same for all police departments, the question of where the effective limits are drawn from department to department must be determined by other than legal and formal criteria. Because this book discusses discretionary decision making that exceeds formally set limits, a specific term is not used to refer to effective limits that are more constricted than are formal limits.

Since the effects that changes in the formal limits have on the effective limits of discretionary behavior are discussed, a modification of the Davis definition is needed. The term *discetionary authority* is used to mean discretion up to the formal limits on discretion as imposed by legislation, court decisions, and (to a lesser extent) administrative policy or rule making. The term *discretionary power* refers to decision making beyond the formal limits; that is, discretionary decision-making practice that falls between formal and effective limits. Discretionary power refers to decisions that officals can and do make with impunity. (Obviously public officials can and occasionally do take bribes, but the taking of bribes is not a discretionary power since negative sanctions generally follow known instances of bribe taking.) The distinction between discretionary authority and discretionary power may be needlessly cumbersome. It may be sufficient to distinguish between authorized and unauthorized discretion. Whichever usage is preferred, it is important that much of the behavior currently labeled as discretionary is actually at variance with the expectations of law. A continuing definitional problem of either discretionary power or unauthorized discretion remains; either may refer to behavior that is expressly prohibited but engaged in nonetheless or to behavior that is merely not authorized.

The granting of relatively broad discretionary authority to public officials is defended on numerous grounds. It is frequently argued that legislative bodies have neither the experience nor the necessary information with which to establish more than a very general framework for decision making. Not only is the legislative body seen as incompetent to prescribe the rules and decisional criteria with sufficient specificity to eliminate substantial discretion, but it is also believed that the political process and its attendant reliance on compromise renders specificity unattainable, even in situations in which competence may be believed to exist. Were legislative enactment the only means of reducing or limiting discretion, this would be a compelling argument.

It is further argued that justice demands that the individual circumstance of each situation require an individualized response. It is therefore thought that a body of rules and decision criteria sufficiently elaborate to attend to the uniqueness of each situation would be impossible to generate and administer. While both opponents and proponents of discretionary authority would agree that similarly situated individuals should be treated similarly, the appropriate criteria for identifying similarly situated individuals is hotly debated. To the classical criminologists, for example, two individuals found guilty of the same offense were similarly situated and consequently deserved similar punishments. According to more contemporary sentencing philosophies, however, two individuals found guilty of the same offense but who differed on one or more of the following dimensions—criminal history, remorse for the offense committed, attitude toward the court, situational specifics of the offense, "dangerousness," need for treatment—would deserve dissimilar punishments. Although one or two additional variables could be handled easily in a preconceived decisional formula, advocates of discretion argue that the number of variables is sufficiently large and their interrelationships sufficiently complex as to preclude the adequate specification of rules in advance.

Central to the position that advocates broad discretionary authority is the faith one places in both the benign intentions and the competence of public decision makers. As long as this trust holds the best that can be expected from predetermined rules and procedure is that they will formally articulate the decisional criteria that have always been informally employed; the worst, of course, is that just and appropriate decisional options will be foreclosed to decision makers.

By the middle of the twentieth century widespread skepticism had emerged regarding the good intentions, competence, and willingness of public officials to confine their decision making within legal bounds. The growth of the civil-rights movement and the belief that race was a significant variable affecting decisional outcome did much to popularize concern about disparity and inequity resulting from the exercise of public discretion by welfare officials, psychiatrists, police, judges, and correctional officials. It became fashionable to believe that not only race but also sex, age, class, demeanor, and attributed moral and personality traits were important variables associated with decisional outcome. The willingness of the Warren court to accept this type of evidence prompted numerous Fourteenth Amendment challenges to existing practice in education, welfare, mental health, and criminal justice. Many, although not all, of these challenges involved the exercise of discretion by public officials. This line of criticism lead critics and many supporters of public human-service systems to seek more structured and less subjective decisional criteria for public organizations.

Closely related criticisms of the "rehabilitative ideal" (Allen 1959), the "therapeutic state" (Kittrie 1971), and of psychiatric and quasi-clinical interventions (Szasz 1963, 1970a, 1970b) brought further questioning of individualized treatment and the discretionary power it has justified. In reference to welfare recipients, mental patients, drug addicts and alcoholics, juvenile delinquents, and (in part) sentenced adult criminals, supporters of the rehabilitative ideal and therapeutic state professed nonpunitive intentions; they alleged a concern for the (re)education, (re)socialization, and general improvement of the client. Francis Allen (1959) was among the first to call this approach into question. (Reprinted by special permission of *The Journal of Criminal Law, Criminology, and Police Science*. Copyright © 1959 by Northwestern University School of Law.)

> [T]he rise of the rehabilitative ideal has often been accompanied by attitudes and measures that conflict, sometimes seriously, with the values of

> individual liberty and volition. . . . The administration of the criminal law presents to any community the most extreme issues of the proper relations of the individual citizen to state power. We are concerned here with the perennial issue of political authority. Under what circumstances is the state justified in bringing its force to bear on the individual human being?

Edelman (1977, p. 60-62) discusses the ways in which the "symbolic" language of the helping professions is mistaken for descriptive language and consequently disguises the coercive and/or punitive consequences of professional action.

> [T]hough the linguistic evocation of the political system is subtle, that very fact frees the participants to act out their political roles blatantly, for they see themselves as helping, not as repressing. . . . The names for forms of mental illness, forms of delinquency, and for educational capacities are the basic terms. Each of them normally involves a high degree of unreliability in diagnosis, in prognosis, and in the prescriptions of rehabilitative treatment; but each also entails unambiguous constraints upon clients, especially their confinement and subjection to the staff and the rules of a prison, school or hospital. The confinement and constraints are converted into liberating and altruistic acts by defining them as education, therapy, or rehabilitation. . . . Regardless of the clinical utility of professional terms, their political utility is manifest; they marshall popular support for professional discretion, concentrating public attention upon procedures and rationalizing in advance any failure of the procedures to achieve their formal objectives.

Recognizing the history and potential for abuse of therapeutic decision making, Kittrie (1971, p. 371) makes the following observation:

> Bowing to the desires and ostensible good-faith opinions of the experts, the law forsook its role as the censor of the exercise of state power and left the therapists to devise their own means for bringing the therapeutic power to bear. Although legislators abetted this process by establishing special and informal administrative procedures for the therapists and appending no safeguards thereto, the absence of procedural safeguards in the therapeutic realm is equally the fault of the courts. They have withheld constitutional protections from putative patients on the basis that the proceedings were noncriminal, and have uncritically accepted the testimony and opinions of doctors, social workers, and others charged with the therapeutic mission. By abridging the individual's right to object and by neglecting to scrutinize the state's requests to exercise therapeutic power, the courts have placed the therapist outside societal controls.

Szasz has long maintained that mental illness is a myth that functions to conceal coercive and punitive attempts to secure moral, ethical, and social conformity under the guise of "scientific" intervention. This line of analysis seeks to clarify the social-control functions implicitly at work in the therapeutic professions. In this connection Szasz has maintained that psychiatry, social work, and other helping professions have as much in common with religion as they have with science. Not only is Szasz offended by this image of moral coercion in the name of science, but he is equally sensitive to the potential class bias reflected in such techniques. In a discussion of nonmedical elements of Soviet medical practice, Szasz (1961, p. 68) addresses this potential.

> [W]ithout wishing to deny the benefits that often accrue to social work clients, this arrangement [state control] clearly empowers the employers to exert a measure of social control—in this case, over members of the lower class. Both systems—that is, Soviet medicine and American social work—are thus admirably suited for the purpose of keeping "in line" potentially discontented members [or groups] of society.

In this discussion of social-work, psychiatric, and therapeutic intervention there is the tacit assumption (it is an explicit assumption in Kittrie 1971) that, unlike the decision situations already listed, the adult criminal justice system functions fully within the bounds of legal expectations and with procedural regularity. Contemporary students of criminal justice, however, have long been dissuaded from this view. Cole (1975, p. 53) observes, "That discretion pervades the administration of justice is obvious." What is less obvious is the extent to which factors thought to be irrelevant or inconsistent to justice play a role in determining the outcome of discretionary decision making.

Every aspect of the criminal-justice system has recently come under extreme criticism for alleged abuses of discretion and for inequity and bias in discretionary decision making. Studies of police practices suggest that the race of suspects and victims plays an important role in determining whether or not the police decide to invoke the criminal process (LaFave 1962; Skolnick 1966; Cochran 1971; Thornberry 1973; Pepinsky 1976). Other studies suggest that the demeanor of suspects toward the police affects their decision to intervene informally, formally, or not at all. (Goldman 1963; LaFave 1965; Piliavin and Briar 1964; Chambliss and Nagasawa 1969; Black and Reiss 1970). Hohenstein (1969) and Black (1970) report that police rely on complainant's wishes when deciding whether or not to arrest. Davis (1975) reports that the Chicago police will not arrest, even in serious crimes such as burglary, robbery, and assault with a deadly weapon, if the victim is available but unwilling to press charges. He maintains that this is true even if the officer observes the crime himself. Research conducted by Terry (1967) and Rubinstein (1973) points to the tendency of police to stereotype certain groups or classes of people as likely suspects and proceed more aggressively against them. Although some studies question the validity of these and other studies imputing police bias, the result of this line of inquiry is increasingly aggressive calls for internal and external review of police discretionary practices.

Studies of bailing practices show that a difference in the racial and socioeconomic status of the defendant affects the ability to make bail (Goldfarb 1965). Ares, Rankin, and Stuez (1963) demonstrate that bail-setting practices of judges frequently differ from public expectations regarding seriousness of offense. This study found a tremendous disparity in dispositions between defendants who were able to secure release on bail and those who were not. Since in many jurisdictions it is the professional bail bondsman and not a court or other law enforcement official who makes the functional decision as to whether a defendant will be released on bail, the inequities in the bail process are seen by some as even more alarming. Although calls for bail reform or alternatives to monetary bail have been frequent over the past ten years and every government study during that period has recommended substantial modification, changes in nationwide release practices have been minimal (Wice 1973).

Green (1961) reviews studies suggesting that extralegal attitudes of judges account for much of the disparity of sentencing. Hagen (1974) reviews many of the theories and studies that have attributed sentencing disparity to extralegal characteristics of either courts or defendants. Both Green and Hagen seek to discredit these assertions, arguing instead that legally appropriate criteria explain most of the observed variance. It appears, however, that their protestations have been insufficient to diminish support for the alternative view. Bullock (1961) claims that the race of the defendant and victim leads to differences in the length of sentence. (Bullock's methodology has been justifiably criticized. The present argument, however, is more concerned with the impact than the accuracy of these observations. Few studies have been more frequently anthologized or cited than Bullock's. In addition, his argument that both more and less punitive sanctions may be applied to minorities is quite suggestive.) Wolfgang (1974) claims that race is the single most important variable in the decision whether or not to invoke the death sentence. Frankel (1973) reviews studies of differences in sentencing practices among jurisdictions and judges within the same jurisdiction. Dershowitz (1976) and Von Hirsh (1976) review arguments pertaining to sentencing disparity and inequity and conclude that determinate sentencing is required to overcome the bias inherent in the exercise of judicial discretion.

Rothman (1971) and Goffman (1961) have offered vivid testimony to the brutal, dehabilitating, and generally unobserved character of "total" institutions. Goldfarb and Singer (1970) observe that "statutes regulating the maintenance and care of prisoners and the power of their keepers to control them are rare. The legislative standards that do exist are vague." Wick (1973), speaking of prison rules and procedures, notes that "the wretched physical conditions pale in importance . . . beside the total arbitrariness of the bureaucracy that rules every aspect of their existence." Fogel (1975) is among the many observers to note that, despite the rehabilitative rhetoric, all prison decisions are dictated by considerations of custody and control. Not only have these observations encouraged pleas for correctional form, but they have also generated suspicion regarding the rehabilitative intentions of decision makers at earlier stages of the criminal justice process.

In reference to parole, O'Leary and Nuffield (1972) report that a nationwide study of parole-board decision making showed that only 43 percent of parole boards directly informed the inmate of their decision, 40 percent made verbatim transcripts of the proceedings, 40 percent permitted counsel at hearings, 31 percent permitted witnesses to appear in behalf of clients at hearings, and 22 percent recorded reasons for their decisions. Sprowls and Bullington (1976) demonstrate that black inmates at a juvenile institution serve longer sentences (controlled for offense) than do white inmates. They argue that inmate demeanor at staffing—the equivalent of parole-release hearings—plus the institutional staff's lack of familiarity with urban, black behavior patterns contribute to these differences. Fogel (1975) suggests that parole decisions are largely based on the inmates' record of institutional adjustment. While this initially seems a reasonable criteria, the absence of transferability between conformity to the artificiality of institutional life and the expectations of life after release renders even this criteria suspect. To the extent that parole decisions rest on attempts to predict dangerousness, current statistical and clinical techniques are grossly inadequate. Studies suggest that modest accuracy can be achieved only at the cost of dramatic overprediction or risk (Von Hirsh 1972; Diamond 1974).

Other studies and arguments seek to disprove that race, class, and other extralegal factors influence official decision making, however, the studies cited have aroused considerable interest and misgiving regarding discretionary decision making. Davis (1969) raises objections of a slightly different nature, contending that most instances of official discretion are not truly discretionary decision making at all. He suggests that once a certain type of decision has been reached several times, decisional criteria are formulated and clarified. The difference between discretionary decision making and the articulation of rules is not what it appears; it is merely the difference between formally specified policy and "secret policy." Seen in this light, discretionary decisions are undesirable because policy is frequently made separately by each official, leading to disparity, rather than being made at the organizational or institutional level; although affected parties could know the content of formal policy, they may only imperfectly be able to guess secret policy; affected parties may never know whether decisions in their particular case represent instances of policy or exceptions to that policy; and it is difficult for affected parties, legislative bodies, courts, and concerned administrative agencies to comment on the desirability of "secret policy," either in its application to a specific case or generally. If genuinely discretionary decision making were being observed, these objections might be the necessary price paid for that form of decision. But if what passes for discretionary decision making is frequently the application of secret policy, the shortcomings are inexcusable.

I am convinced that current opposition to broad discretionary power entrusted to public officials is a result of the allegations I have made. If faith in the good intentions, competence, and wisdom of discretionary decision making had not been undermined in this manner, the question of rule of law versus discretion would be moot. This faith has been significantly shaken, and there is a desire to control, constrain, limit, or eliminate discretion from numerous decision points.

Conventional wisdom has frequently seen formal rules as inhibitive of individual interest in dealing with the state. This, of course, is often the case. But rules also inhibit official action in the interest of protecting the individual. The merit of rules in this capacity has only recently been broadly appreciated.

The definitions of discretion contend that discretion is exercised within legal bounds, is not capricious or unrestrained, is based on fact and guided by law, represents a responsible choice, and rests on an understanding of what is lawful, right, or wise. Because these definitions are incompatible with the images of discretionary decision making examined thus far, proposals to reduce or eliminate discretion have been generated.

Davis (1969) reviews the historic arguments against the exercise of discretion by public officials; he labels this argument the "extravagant version of the rule of law." This position seeks to eliminate discretion through one of two means. The first of these suggests that all action by government officials be controlled by predetermined law. Thus the legislature is required to specify the parameters of decision situations, criteria to be employed, and alternative decisional outcomes appropriate to each situation. Administrators are only supposed to apply the law as it is given. The second position is slightly more moderate. While it tacitly recognizes that preestablished rule may be insufficient to determine appropriate official action, it demands that legal rights be determined by regularly constituted courts. In this regard Dickerson (1927) offers a typical argument (quoted in Davis 1969).

> Nothing has been held more fundamental to the supremacy of law than the right of every citizen to bring the action of government officials to trial in the ordinary courts of the common law. That government officials, on the contrary, should themselves assume to perform the functions of a law court and determine the rights of individuals, as is the case under a system of administrative justice, has traditionally been felt to be inconsistent with the supremacy of law. . . . In short, every citizen is entitled, first, to have his rights adjudicated in a regular common-law court, and, secondly, to call into question in such a court the legality of any act done by an administrative official.

Hayek (1960), in a more contemporary though no less extravagant approach, combines the two positions (quoted in Davis 1969).

> The rule of law means that government must never coerce an individual except in the enforcement of a known rule. . . . Under the rule of law, government can infringe a person's protected private sphere only as a punishment for breaking an announced general rule. . . . The rule of law requires that the executive in its coercive action be bound by rules which prescribe not only when and where it may use coercion but also in what manner it

> may do so. . . . The decision must be deductible from the rules of law and from those circumstances to which the law refers and which can be known to the parties concerned. The decision must not be affected by any special knowledge possessed by the government or by its momentary purposes and the particular value it attaches to different concrete aims, including the preferences it may have concerning the effects on different people.

Hayek concedes that considerable discretion must be granted to administrative agencies. Where this is inevitable and unavoidable, he contends that such discretion "must be controlled by the possibility of a review of the substance of the decision by an independent court." Here the court must determine "whether the law provided for a particular action that an authority has undertaken."

If discretionary authority were not granted to governmental or public officials as rule of law-supremacy of law advocates have instructed, it is difficult to imagine what modern government would be. Surely the legislatures and the courts had neither the competence nor the inclination to attend with specificity to all the requirements of contemporary governmental decision making. One is disinclined to suspect that the results would be particularly admirable if they had tried. But even if they tried, and tried aggressively, surely discretion could not be eliminated. Davis (1969) suggests that by so elaborately overstating their case they may have inadvertently contributed to the growth rather than the reduction of discretion.

> My opinion is that, paradoxically, today's excessive discretionary power is largely attributable to the zeal of those who a generation or two ago were especially striving to protect against excessive discretionary power. If they had been less zealous they would have attempted less, and if they had attempted less they might have succeeded. They attempted too much—so much that they could not possibly succeed—and they were soundly defeated. They tended to oppose all discretionary power; they should have opposed only unnecessary discretionary power.

What is equally paradoxical is the frequency with which the observation that all discretion could not and should not be eliminated leads observers to conclude that it is undesirable or impossible to control any discretion. Only recently have some commentators treated discretion not as an either-or issue but as a matter of balance between two potentially compatible rather than mutually exclusive forces. These more modest proposals contend that discretion may be reduced, limited, structured, controlled, reallocated, or otherwise changed through a number of means.

Strategies for Reducing Discretion

Davis (1969) contends that statutory changes need not and probably cannot play a significant role in reducing discretion, however, his contempt for the legislature's willingness and potential ability to control discretion may be unwarranted. Clearly there are numerous things that legislative bodies are generally disinclined and ill suited to do. It seems unlikely, for instance, that they will produce satisfactory specific criteria for decision making. However, it is likely that legislative prohibition of certain decisional outcomes or options might be very successful at limiting discretion. For example, decriminalization of victimless crimes would do much to reduce discretion in criminal justice, particularly among the police. Davis (1969) is right that legislatures are unlikely to do this. By abdicating responsibility for keeping criminal legislation current and continuing to overlegislate, legislative bodies have not only permitted but compelled police and prosecutors to attempt to make the criminal law reasonable and just through the exercise of discretion. If the only available choices were between current discretionary excesses and a policy of full enforcement of existing criminal laws, it would be wise to opt to suffer the abuses of discretion.

There is the suspicion that standards, guidelines, or criteria for decision making imposed by the legislature would be more objectionable than current discretionary practices. Regarding criminal sentencing, there exists considerable and well-founded concern that proposals for mandatory sentences imposed by statutes may prove to be unconscionably punitive. For whatever reason there is relatively little discussion of the role of legislative bodies in the control of discretion in the theoretical and prescriptive literature. Legislatures could have a profound impact on the exercise of official discretion, and in some instances have tried to do so.

A more popular response in the literature to the problem of discretional abuse is through recourse to adjudication and judicial review. Reich (1963, 1964, 1965, 1966) considers the role of official discretion in the distribution of government largess, particularly welfare benefits. Reich was among the leaders of the effort to change the image of welfare benefits as a "privilege" extended voluntarily by the state. Reich and others maintained that these benefits are the "rights" of eligible citizens and as such could not be withdrawn except through due process of law. Reich (1964) maintained that these rights were the "new property" and required protections comparable to property rights.

Over the past ten to fifteen years tremendous advances have been made as a result of efforts to clarify the rights of clients of public agencies and officials. The welfare-rights movement has secured considerable protections for welfare recipients against extralegal denial or termination of welfare benefits. Courts have sought to regulate the involuntary commitment of the mentally ill. During the 1960s the Warren court extended these and similar protections to citizens under arrest, on parole, in court, correctional institutions, and juvenile court. These changes have been of sufficient magnitude to lead Cole (1975) to refer to this trend as the due-process revolution.

The impact of these court victories has not always secured the protections that their advocates had envisioned or the court had mandated. From situation to situation differing degrees of circumvention were frequently possible; sometimes absolute noncompliance resulted. Jowell (1975) notes the problem of differential access to administrative or judicial review. Those who wish to see the due-process revolution continue are fearful that the new composition of the Supreme Court since the mid-1970s will no longer be receptive to such strategies. In fact, there has already been some movement in the current court to reverse itself with reference to exclusionary rules. These difficulties notwithstanding, the due-process revolution has not only left its mark on the relationship between public officials and citizens and clients but has also, and more importantly, set the stage for further challenges to official discretion. Aside from questions of their immediate impact, these Supreme Court decisions have played an important symbolic role in questioning the appropriateness of the decision making of public officials.

The most fashionable recommended strategy for reducing discretion is through administrative rule making. Davis (1969) continues to be the most visible proponent of this strategy. Drawing heavily on the provisions of the Administrative Procedures Act, Davis (1969, 1975) advocates the following reforms:

1. "Secret policy" is to be avoided in preference for formal, public policy. Policy should be as specific as the particular decision situation permits. This policy need not be inviolate; exceptions would be permissible if accompanied by written reasons.

2. Proposed policy or rules should be distributed for comment to affected parties or their representatives. It goes without saying that there is an expectation that reactions of affected parties be considered in good faith.
3. Reasons for particular decisions should always be provided to affected parties.
4. Except where the potential harm of such action is manifest, decisions should be public.
5. Not only must rules be clarified but "superior officers must enforce more strictly against subordinates; federal officials must enforce more strictly against state officials."

Davis maintains that such practices would not only allow for greater visibility of decision making by affected parties—including the general public—but would also make questionable decisions and practices more amenable to judicial review. For example, police have informal or secret policy regarding arrest for low visibility, minor criminal-law infractions. In many instances the informal policy is not to arrest. However, if for extralegal reasons the police choose to arrest an individual for such a violation, the observation, even if accompanied by elaborate proof, that others are not arrested for this offense is insufficient as a defense. Were the policy of nonenforcement for that offense official department policy, however, a defense would at least be possible. The minimum expectation at a review is that the police justify their departure from policy. These procedures, with the ensuing prospect of review, could reasonably be expected to reduce harassment arrests. But it is precisely because the police frequently see harassment arrests as an important ingredient in their order-maintenance task that they are likely to oppose the type of reform suggested by Davis.

Davis (1969, 1975) is firmly committed to the belief that administrative rule making seeking to confine and control the exercise of discretion is in the interest of the organization as much as that of the client. He is willing to concede, however, that many organizations will fail to perceive this fact. Because the rule-making task may not be voluntarily undertaken, Davis contends that such activities should be ordered by the court. Unfortunately Davis does not consider the problems associated with soliciting good-faith compliance with such court orders.

Davis (1969) draws heavily on examples from federal regulatory agencies and the Administrative Procedures Act for his discussion of discretion. He contends that much recent progress has been made in those areas and proposes them as models for reform in other administrative organizations. Davis implicitly acknowledges that the high status and the political, economic, and legal resources of clients of federal regulatory agencies may be significant variables explaining the success with which these clients have been able to win protections against discretionary actions by officials charged with their regulation. Without further argument or examples, one is hesitant to accept on faith the assertion that the tactics and procedures that may have rescued major corporations from excessive discretionary action by public officials will be equally successful at safeguarding the interests of the poor, powerless, and disrespectable.

Davis offers a less than convincing argument, but most other prescriptive proposals offer none. The literature on discretion has so far not attended to that literature assessing the compliance with or impact of court decisions or statutory requirements relating to official action. The studies of compliance and impact offer insight into how the various tactics and proposals for controlling discretion may be responded to by public decision makers.

Compliance and Impact

Until recently there was the generalized assumption that public officials, unlike private citizens, behave as the law expects. Critics of bureaucracy were convinced that overzealous and unquestioning subservience to rules by bureaucratic officials was among the major shortcomings of that organizational form. Lately, however, numerous studies have been addressed to the discrepancies between authorative pronouncements and actual official behavior. The majority of this literature concerns itself with the impact of Supreme Court decisions.

Unfortunately most of these studies are descriptive rather than theoretical and focus on very specific points of law. The result is that they are of only limited utility in guiding future efforts. Although they do not answer the necessary questions, they at least provide a starting point.

Implicit in many of these studies is the distinction between compliance and impact, although that distinction is rarely clearly drawn. For instance, in a study of 121 school districts in Tennessee, Birkby (1966) studied the consequences of the Schempp decision in which the Supreme Court held that required devotional exercises in public schools were forbidden. Birkby found that of the 121 districts, 70 had done nothing to comply, 50 had changed policy so that individual classroom teachers decided whether or not to conduct classroom devotional exercises, and only 1 had eliminated such exercises. It is clear that in the 1 district that eliminated devotional exercises there was both compliance and impact. One might argue, however, that this district overcomplied, since it is far from clear that the court either required or intended that devotional exercises be completely discontinued. In Birkby's view 51 districts complied: the 50 that changed their policy and the 1 that discontinued devotional exercises. He acknowledges, however, that the change in policy produced no change in actual practice. While there may have been compliance, there is no indication of impact. It is doubtful that the court intended such a trivial outcome.

Medalie, Zeitz, and Alexander (1968) report a study of the implementation of *Miranda* in Washington, D.C., in which lawyers were available in the station house on a twenty-four-hours-a-day, seven-days-a-week basis (Precinct Representation Project). These lawyers were volunteers to the project and in no way connected to the police department. The authors report that only 7 percent of the suspects brought to the precinct opted for project lawyers and 40 percent of suspects who were advised of their rights nonetheless gave statements to the police. From subsequent interviews with suspects from this population, the authors conclude that a considerable number of suspects either partially or completely misunderstood their rights. On the basis of these and other findings noted in the study, they conclude: "In light of the foregoing data on police practices under Miranda and the defendants' response, even in an optimum system of precinct representation, with well-trained counsel at the police station available as soon as the defendant is brought in, the odds against even beginning to approach the model established by the court in *Miranda* would have been exceedingly high." In an observational study conducted in New Haven (Yale Law Journal 1967), the author concludes that the manner in which rights are read to suspects can encourage disbelief in their sincerity and even imply a threat of reprisal should such rights be exercised.

While both studies indicate instances in which suspects were not informed of their rights or were not informed in a timely fashion, such incidents were relatively rare. If informing suspects of their rights constitutes compliance, compliance with *Miranda* was high, although not complete. The authors in both studies, however, are clearly of the opinion that outcome and practice fell short of the results envisioned in *Miranda*. Since it is unlikely that the court intended that all suspects be represented by counsel, even against their wishes, and that no suspects make statements to the police, even if they wished to do so, a good deal of judgment is required to determine what impact the court intended.

Seeburger and Wettick (1967), in a study of the impact of the *Miranda* decision in the detective branch of the Pittsburgh police department, announce that within one week after the court's decision, detectives were informing suspects of their rights. Unfortunately the authors fail to provide a description of the manner in which information regarding rights was imparted. The authors conclude that the consequences of *Miranda* were that confession rates dropped from 54.4 percent pre-*Miranda* to 37.5 percent post-*Miranda* for homicides, robberies, burglaries, auto larcenies, and forceable rapes. Although the court did not decide *Miranda* with the objective of reducing confessions and making the job of police, prosecutors, and courts more difficult, this outcome is logically related to consequences the court did seek to achieve. Although this is clearly an impact of *Miranda*, it is dramatically inconsistent with the impact that Medalie, Zeitz, and Alexander (1968) explored.

Stapleton and Teitlebaum (1973) and Canon and Kolson (1971) conclude that in some jurisdictions juveniles who opt to exercise their right to counsel are given more negative sanctions than similarly situated juveniles who choose not to be represented. Surely this is incompatible with the intent of the court. It is a right of dubious value that secures for its possessor penalties rather than protections; and yet there is compliance (the lawyer was present), and there is impact (a difference in disposition).

Thus impact could occur in the absence of compliance. A hypothetical example follows, chosen from the study to be considered in detail later. Recent Pennsylvania law requires that detention hearings be held for juveniles within seventy-two hours, however, such hearings are rarely held. If data on length of detention from a year predating the statute were compared with comparable data for a post-statute year and that data indicated the length of time in detention had been significantly reduced, one might hypothesize that the code had an impact on the length of detention, even though there was total noncompliance with the requirement of the statute. (It is obvious that factors unrelated to the statute might better explain the reduction.)

In an effort to avoid conceptual confusions, the following terms will be employed throughout the remainder of this book:

Noncompliance means failure to adhere to the specific requirements of a statute, court decision, or administrative rule.

Technical compliance means observance of the letter of the law without apparent regard for the spirit or intent of the requirement.

Substantial compliance means observance of the letter of the law and an apparently successful effort to observe the spirit or intent of the requirement.

Residual impact means those consequences of a requirement not central to its intent.

These definitions are not without their difficulties. The language of statutes and court decisions is frequently imprecise and unspecific, permitting interpretation of the actions necessary to achieve technical compliance. (The definition of substantial compliance is such that its meaning will always be ambiguous and imprecise.) The phrases "all deliberate speed" in *Brown* v. *Board of Education* (Sarratt 1971) and "maximum feasible participation" in the Office of Economic Opportunity (O.E.O.) legislation (Moynihan 1969) are among the most well-known examples of this type of language. Such nonspecific, ambiguous language has its obvious merits in situations requiring compromise and consensus. It is clear that Chief Justice Earl Warren, in drafting the court's decision in *Brown* v. *Board of Education*, chose to purchase unanimity at the price of specificity. In the case of the maximum-feasible-participation clause, ambiguity may be the result of sheer inadvertence: in Moynihan's phrase, the result of "maximum feasible misunderstanding." While the efficacy of ambiguity is undeniable in consensus-building and decision-making situations, its contribution to confusion, deliberate and accidental misunderstanding, circumvention, and delay at the stage of implementation and compliance is equally irrefutable. This dilemma is not easily resolved, since narrow margins of victory in the legislature and on the court have a similar effect (Murphy 1959). One of the clearest hypotheses that can be drawn is that the more ambiguous the language of the requirement, the greater the noncompliance. Although noncompliance is such situations may result from good-faith misunderstandings of the requirements imposed by ambiguous language, the inclination is to view such noncompliance or circumvention as deliberate.

Response to the Supreme Court decision in *Brown* v. *Board of Education*, first in the South and later throughout the nation, occasioned considerable interest in compliance with Supreme Court rulings. This is not the first instance in which the court's difficulty in obtaining compliance was noted. In 1832, President Andrew Jackson is alleged to have said of a Supreme Court decision pertaining to a dispute between the Cherokee nation and the state of Georgia that "John Marshall has made his decision; now let him enforce it." *Brown* v. *Board of Education* occasioned the first of a series of social-science investigations of the specifics of compliance. In 1963, nine years after the decision, only 1 percent of southern, black students were attending school with whites. Although that number climbed to 25 percent by 1968, observers wondered whether or not such compliance was consistent with the court's admonition to proceed with all deliberate speed.

Much early attention—1954 through the mid-1960s—focused on the southern federal bench (Peltason 1961; Vines 1964). Recent attention to desegregation has been national, with increasingly more divergent variables taken into consideration. While this broadening of perspective has contributed immensely to a greater understanding of desegration, it has unfortunately focused attention away from the specific issue of compliance. There is little doubt that the involvement of federal administrative agencies, through their control of federal funds, exerted tremendous pressure on local authorities to move to end segregation. The need for administrative support to enforce judicial and legislative decisions is clear. The nature of this relationship and manner in which this executive support is engaged have not been examined extensively.

Neither judicial nor legislative orders are necessarily self-initiating. Of central interest is the discovery of which conditions if any are prerequisite to compliance. Executive orders are more likely to elicit prompt compliance because the executive has direct authority over parties who are expected to comply. Neusadt (1960), however, clearly demonstrates that executive orders are at best only self-initiating under a limited set of conditions. He suggests that an order must have at least the following five characteristics if it is to be self-executing: the issuer of the order must be unambiguously involved in making the decision, the order must be unambiguously worded, the order must receive wide publicity, those receiving the order must have control of the means of implementation, and there must be no doubt of the individual's authority to issue the order. Even executive orders that meet these five criteria are not necessarily self-executing.

The necessity or sufficiency of the above criteria have not been subjected to careful testing. Even if the validity of these hypotheses were confirmed, their transferability to legislative or judicial expectations would be problematic. These hypotheses presuppose a direct line of authority that would be suspect with respect to administrative compliance with legislative or judicial orders. Here, it may be necessary to identify a situationally specific enforcement mechanism that functions as a surrogate to the executive's presumed control of those directly accountable to him. The exclusionary rule is such a mechanism with respect to court expectations regarding due process and procedural regularity in criminal proceedings. Although such power may be tacitly assumed, it is interesting that Neustadt does not consider directly sanctioning possibilities that follow noncompliance. At least with regard to executive orders, it may be assumed that dismissal or being passed over for promotion may be a consequence of failure to comply. It is not clear, however, what if any penalties may follow noncompliance with many legislative or judicial expectations.

Many recent studies of the consequences of legislation have also begun to express a more aggressive skepticism about the relationship between formal statutory expectations and actual outcomes. The majority of these studies concentrated on O.E.O. and comparable human-service legislation (Moynihan 1969; Pressman and Wildavsky 1973). Researchers have concluded that the impact of these programs has fallen substantially short of what they presume the legislative intent was. Research of this nature has come to be referred to as implementation studies; but in many respects it is similar to impact studies of Supreme Court decisions. They are only partially relevant to the study of compliance, however. Since the question of technical compliance is generally a minor issue in implementation studies, the utility of the literature is restricted to concerns specific to substantial compliance.

As in the studies of compliance with court decisions, the impression of most researchers is that officials willfully and successfully sought to avoid substantial compliance. Because legislative language in this area focuses on intended consequences for target populations rather than on specific behavioral expectations for public officials (as is the case with most compliance studies), attempts to integrate the two obviously related areas of study are easily frustrated. It is also possible that compliance differs between situations in which new, additional behaviors are required, as is the case in this legislation, and situations in which previous practices are forbidden, which has generally been the case with court decisions.

The compliance literature fails in many important respects to concern itself with dynamics of compliance. Researchers have selected high-noncompliance areas for study; consequently they have observed noncompliance rather than compliance. This documentation of noncompliance has drawn attention to profound political and moral questions regarding government's ability to regulate its own conduct. But the documentation of the extent and pervasiveness of noncompliance has not yet contributed much to understanding the dynamics of noncompliance. Because attention has been focused on high-noncompliance situations, the factors associated with official compliance have not been explored.

Davis (1969) frequently cites the impact of the Administrative Procedures Act on reducing the discretion of federal regulatory agencies. He maintains that officials of federal regulatory agencies have complied with provisions of the Administrative Procedures Act, which limits their discretionary authority. A review of the examples provided by Davis, however, indicates that only agency ability to pursue courses of action which subjects of the agency's authority perceived to be inconsistent with their self-interest was limited. That major corporations, the typical subject of federal regulatory agency activity in Davis's examples, are able to defend their interests against the improper exercise of regulatory agency discretion is not surprising. The assumption that welfare recipients, mental patients, criminal suspects, convicted felons, or juvenile offenders similarly would be able to defend their self-interest were comparable legislation extant in those areas may be unwarranted. Yet this is Davis's assertion.

Jowell (1975) studied the impact of open hearings and public decision making and appeal-process requirements imposed on three administrative agencies in the Boston area. He examined the welfare appeals process, discrimination complaints (Massachusetts Commission against Discrimination), and citizen participation in urban renewal. He concluded that the differential resources and consequent access to political influence and legal assistance of various interest groups was the principal variable affecting restraints on administrative discretion.

The findings presented by Jowell are in most respects similar to those abstracted from Davis. In both instances the success with which compliance is achieved or discretion is limited must be seen as a consequence of the power, resources, and influence of affected parties. Neither Jowell nor Davis seem to be aware of the implications of this observation. Enforcement is not usually viewed as a private individual or group responsibility; yet by default that appears to be the case in these examples. Public responsibility for enforcement is either lacking or ineffective. Given the inequity of the distribution of resources among parties affected by governmental decision making, the inadequacies of such a state of affairs does not require further comment.

Where studies of discretion and compliance have gone beyond documenting the extent of discretion and noncompliance, their attention has focused on characteristics of either subjects of official decisions or of official decision makers. Frequently hypotheses regarding noncompliance are no more sophisticated than those advanced by Wasby (1970) and Muir (1962), who suggest that officials comply with expectations which agree with their personal ideologies more frequently than with those expectations they oppose. All things being equal, such an observation is tautologically self-evident. However, at least occasionally, officials comply with expectations they aggressively oppose, and they sometimes fail to comply with expectations against which they have no personal bias. It would be bizarre to suggest that personal characteristics of decision makers and their subjects are of no consequence in determining the outcome of decisions. Recent organizational literature provides numerous reasons to believe that organizational and environmental factors provide more satisfactory explanations of behavior than do the personal characteristics of individuals (Perrow 1970; Thompson 1967; Kast and Rosenzweig 1973).

In what may become a seminal study in criminal justice, Eisenstein and Jacob (1977) examine the disposition of felony cases in three cities: Baltimore, Chicago, and Detroit. Unlike in more conventional studies of court decision-making and sentencing practices, they explain differences in disposition as a result of the characteristics of court organization and sponsoring organizations. The principal explanatory variable employed is the stability of courtroom workgroups; stable workgroups are those in which the same judge, representative of the prosecutor's office, and representative of the defender's office are assigned to the same courtroom for extended periods. Eisenstein and Jacob demonstrate that, among other things, the point at which cases were disposed of in the criminal court process was primarily determined by the stability or instability of the workgroup. They additionally call attention to specific organizational and ideological characteristics of defender organizations. They establish that the nature of funding and reimbursement practices affects the nature of defense behavior.

By seeking to explain court behavior in organizational terms rather than as a consequence of personal characteristics of the defendant or the decision maker, Eisenstein and Jacob provide a model with which discretion and compliance may be profitably studied, even though they do not deal with these topics directly. (Despite pronounced differences in subject matter and methodology, the conceptual perspective developed in the following chapters is indebted to the Eisenstein and Jacob study.)

Davis's work (1969) represents the first and only major theoretical examination of discretion (even though it is actually more accurately described as prescriptive rather than theoretical), and Wasby's work (1970) remains the first and only ambitious theoretical treatment of compliance. Unfortunately, however, Wasby does not provide a general theory. Instead he reviews earlier research and attempts to accumulate potential hypotheses. The 136 hypotheses presented are often contradictory, frequently confusing with respect to the direction of causality, and sometimes so mundane that their theoretical utility is suspect.

Among the hypotheses suggested by Wasby (1970, p. 246-266), the following are most useful when considering compliance with legislatively imposed expectations. His hypotheses pertaining to compliance with Supreme Court decisions must be assumed to be transferable to other compliance situations.

1. Decisions limiting government action will provide more immediate reaction than those upholding or legitimating such action.
2. Compliance will be more immediate when courts provide clear guidelines than when they do not.

3. Ambiguity in Supreme Court rulings decreases compliance.
4. Ambiguity in a decision increases the influence of local values in the resolution of conflict in the aftermath of a decision.
5. Decisions released simultaneously with other decisions are less likely to have impact than decisions released separately.
6. Inadequate transmission of court decisions will reduce support for and understanding of the court.
7. The longer a law has been in effect, the more unwilling legislators will be to discard the practice it embodies.
8. Compliance is less likely when statutory requirements for a practice exist than when they are absent.
9. If an interest group is highly organized and has resources, it will be more likely to follow through to protect its interests than if it is not so organized and does not have resources.
10. The greater the centralization of an organization, the greater the compliance with court decisions.
11. The more persistent the enforcers are, the greater the compliance.
12. Compliance is more likely when some reviewing body is available to those complaining of noncompliance.
13. Units of government are less likely to comply with court rulings than are individuals.
14. Judges are more likely to follow Supreme Court opinion than are other governmental officials.
15. Those seeking higher office in the judicial system will be more likely to comply with Supreme Court decisions than those in other positions.
16. The greater the range of policy matters with which an official is involved, the less likely he will be to comply with a Supreme Court decision.
17. The greater the discretion of local officials, the lower the compliance with Supreme Court rulings.
18. The smaller the community, the more closely local officials must follow local values in reacting to court decisions.

Conclusion

A review of the tables of contents and indexes of law or criminal justice texts published before the mid-1960s reveal only the most incidental reference to discretion. In more recent texts discretion is frequently a major theme. The civil-rights movement, the distrust of official government action occasioned by Vietnam and Watergate, and social-science studies suggesting the existence of extralegal disparity in official decisional outcomes have resulted in increased questioning of the equity and appropriateness of broad discretionary power in the hands of public officials. The past fifteen years have witnessed numerous legislative and court actions intended to delimit the discretionary authority of public officials. The revisions of procedures for the civil commitment of the mentally ill and eligibility criteria for welfare recipients have been particularly dramatic. More recently criminal-justice practices, particularly with respect to sentencing and granting parole, have come under attack. Practices in the juvenile court, where discretionary power is the most pervasive, face ever-increasing criticism. As faith in both the competence and benign intentions of public decision makers has been shaken, various proposals have been advanced seeking to curtail official discretionary authority.

Contemporary to the growth of concern about alleged abuses of official discretion has been the growing realization that legislative, executive, and judicial decisions are not necessarily self-initiating. Even a casual observation of official response to the Supreme Court decision in *Brown* v. *Board of Education* indicates that circumvention, delay, and outright noncompliance are potential official responses to such decisions. Encouraged by the response, or nonresponse, of public officials to the court's decisions, a number of studies assess the nature of official compliance (Johnson 1967; Wasby 1970). Frequently these studies are referred to as impact studies (Becker and Feeley 1973).

Without underestimating the importance of discretion and compliance studies, it is necessary to examine their shortcomings. First, the overwhelming majority of the work in these areas has been empirical and descriptive rather than theoretical. Although the work of Davis (1969) and Wasby (1970) are exceptions, Davis's treatment of discretion is more prescriptive than theoretical, and Wasby's examination of compliance suggests so many potential hypotheses that one wonders whether these contradictory and unrelated hypotheses are particularly instructive either as guides to theory generation or further empirical research. Not only have the studies undertaken thus far been primarily atheoretical, they have also been conducted in areas where discretionary power was known to be high and noncompliance was extensive. One is therefore likely to learn much about the extent of noncompliance but little about compliance, much about the pervasiveness of discretion and little about its control. (Even in the bureaucracy literature that frequently attends to compliance and rule observation, there exists the clear presumption that such compliance as is noted is dysfunctional rather than desirable.)

In addition observers of discretion are generally opposed to official discretion; the compliance literature has been written by those who are opposed to noncompliance in the area under examination. It would be interesting, but currently impossible, to read an account of compliance and noncompliance in *Brown* v. *Board of Education* from the segregationist perspective.

Second, while discretion and noncompliance are by no means synonymous, there is a clear relationship between the two in numerous contexts. Wasby (1970) does suggest in one of his numerous hypotheses that officials with extensive discretionary powers are better able to avoid compliance than are officials with less discretion. With this exception, however, the literatures on discretion and compliance have developed separately, with little evidence that one is aware of the other's existence. This may result from failure to clearly distinguish between authority granted to the decision maker by statute, administrative ruling, or some other form of delegation and authority usurped by the decision maker in defiance of existing statutory expectation or ruling. Davis (1969) is one of the few voices calling attention to the fact that the majority of currently objectional or problematic discretionary decision making is of this latter variety. It would be just as appropriate to refer to this type of decision making as lawlessness or noncompliance. Students interested in the control or regulation of discretionary powers through legislation, court decisions, or administrative policy have not acknowledged that continued exercise of discretion in the face of formal prohibition is noncompliance. On the other hand, students of compliance rarely acknowledge that compliance almost always presupposes an externally imposed limitation on decisional criteria, behavior, and outcome. Generally compliance suggests a diminution of autonomy. The reader's mind might turn to legislation, court decisions, or administrative policy that enlarges the scope of decisional or behavioral options available. Although one might speak of implementation or impact with regard to such situations, the term compliance would be inappropriate if such expanded options were only made available. If additional behaviors are mandated, however, that too constitutes a limitation; in this context, there is no difference between one must and one must not.

Not all attempts to secure compliance are attempts to reduce discretion. There is, however, a clear relationship between the two. Students of compliance have failed to realize that the intent, or at least the inevitable consequence, of many of the statutes, court decisions, and administrative rulings that they study is to reduce discretionary power. Given the similarity of concerns and the frequency of overlap, it is surprising that students of discretion have so infrequently attended to compliance and students of compliance have so seldom concerned themselves with discretion.

The final, and perhaps most unfortunate, shortcoming of the discretion and compliance studies is that there is a sense in which they are not really studies of discretion or compliance at all. Most empirical studies of discretion deal exclusively with the ways in which the demographic charcteristics of one outcome grouping differ from those of an alternative grouping; that is, the demeanor of those arrested as opposed to the demeanor of those not arrested, the race of those sentenced as opposed to the race of those not sentenced, and so forth. Having discovered the ways in which outcome groupings differ, the researchers infer that these factors were the decisional criteria employed by the decision maker. These inferences explain very little about the dynamics and functions of discretion. Why are these criteria employed rather than more apparently legitimate criteria? What individual or organizational advantages accrue to the application of these rather than alternative criteria? Why do decision makers in some organizational contexts apparently seek to accumulate discretionary power while those in other contexts are inclined to avoid discretionary decision-making responsibility? What changes in legal, organizational, or extraorganizational factors might be related to changes in the decisional criteria applied?

The discretion literature has attended to characteristics of decision situations rather than to characteristics of clients or subjects of the decisional process, but analysis generally has been restricted to demographic and personality characteristics of decision makers. Efforts in this area have centered on attempts to identify tendencies of decision-making types—classified by education, years of experience, personal ideology, and class—to arrive at certain decisional outcomes. While these findings may be interesting in their own right, they contribute little toward understanding how decisional outcomes might be changed or manipulated. It is clearly either impossible or extremely difficult to change or control the types of decision-maker characteristics that have been studied thus far. Discretion studies have documented the inequity and inappropriateness of much official decision making and demonstrated the need for substantial reform. They have contributed little, however, to an understanding of how such reform might be effected.

Pulling together reliable conclusions or even identifying reputable hypotheses from such an unsystematic body of literature is problematic. For purposes of examination of discretion and compliance in the juvenile court, the following guiding assumptions are drawn from the existing literature.

1. The ability of government to control its own behavior has emerged as a widely disputed issue. Studies of discretion and compliance have demonstrated the lack of correspondence between official, formal, and legal pronouncements and actual official behavior so that discretion and compliance may be said to have the status of a social problem. Although the literatures on discretion and compliance have developed separately, closer examination reveals that noncompliance frequently results from efforts to structure, control, or otherwise reduce official discretion. Clearly this is the case with respect to recent efforts to reform the juvenile court.

2. Stategies have been proposed to reduce or control discretion; presumably these same strategies are equally applicable to efforts to obtain compliance, although the compliance literature has not been so prescriptive. These strategies involve either statutory regulation, judicial challenge, or administrative rule making. Thus far these strategies have been proposed separately as if either one were sufficient in and of itself to prompt desired results. It seems, however, that neither will independently result in reduced discretion or increased compliance; This book examines the interrelationship between legislative, judicial, and administrative behavior with respect to discretion and compliance of Pennsylvania Juvenile Court officials.

3. If anything emerges clearly from the compliance literature, it is that vague, ambiguous language invites noncompliance. If language is sufficiently precise and unambiguous, the compliance literature assumes that at least technical compliance will result. With reference to legislative expectations recently imposed on the Pennsylvania Juvenile Court, statutory language concerning certain options available to court decision makers could not be more clear. Everything in the compliance literature (plus common sense) would predispose one to anticipate technical compliance. The statutory lan-

guage, however, is extremely unclear about what the long-term consequences for clients are to be. As a result of this ambiguity with respect to outcome, it is appropriate to anticipate the relative absence of substantial compliance.

4. Both conventional wisdom and much of the compliance literature anticipate relatively high judicial compliance. Such an assumption is unwarranted particularly with respect to the juvenile court, whose history has been one of unfettered decisional authority and power. It is interesting that such behavior is unseemly of those public officials who appear to take the greatest delight in informing disgruntled citizens that the law is the law and must be obeyed until such time as it is changed. It is fascinating how little faith judges apparently place in their own advice.

5. The emphasis in discretion and compliance studies on personal, demographic characteristics of clients and decision makers in explaining official behavior or misbehavior has been shown. A need exists to examine discretion and compliance in terms of organizationally and environmentally relevant variables.

4 A Preliminary Study of Juvenile-Court Compliance

The response of selected Pennsylvania juvenile courts to the provisions of the state's revised Juvenile Court Act (1972) are assessed here. Attention is also directed to the impact of United States Supreme Court decisions but only on the basis of general observational and interview data and to the extent relevant to juvenile-court compliance with legislative provisions.

Specifically the focus is on court compliance with the following expectations of the Juvenile Court Act: seventy-two-hour detention hearing, five-day limit on detention in a county jail, ten-day adjudicatory hearing, use of detention centers or shelter-care facilities rather than the county jail, and six-month review and twelve-month dispositional review hearing.

The Study

The information presented in this and subsequent chapters originates in approximately equal parts from conventional data collection methods, espionage, and serendipity. During the fall of 1976, I was contacted by staff of the commissioner of children and youth, the Department of Public Welfare, about participating in a two- to three-month study of detention practices in the Pennsylvania juvenile courts. At that time neither I nor anyone else involved with the study was familiar with the compliance literature. The study was not purposefully planned or implemented as a study of either discretion or compliance, although its relationship to the issue of judicial discretion was tacitly acknowledged. Instruments were designed and the survey executed unaided by either guiding theoretical assumptions or a review of any of the relevant literature. It was only after the survey was completed that I recognized the basis for a discretion and compliance study.

The commissioner of children and youth, Dr. Jerome Miller, had previously closed all juvenile institutions in Massachusetts (Ohlin, Coates, and Miller 1974; Rutherford 1974; Miller and Ohlin 1976).

He went to Pennsylvania at the request of the governor, after a brief stay in Illinois, and was instrumental in closing the State Correctional Institution at Camp Hill to further juvenile referrals (Sprowls and Bullington 1976). I was involved in a study of the effort to remove juveniles from the Camp Hill facility (Sprowls and Bullington 1976), was extremely interested in Miller's reform tactics and strategies, and modestly curious about the invisible internal functioning of the juvenile courts. My initial interest in the project was motivated primarily by a desire to observe Miller in action and secondarily by an interest in juvenile-court record-keeping and decision-making practices. Questions regarding the differential treatment afforded criminal versus status offenders were of no direct interest.

Not surprisingly, Miller's reputation preceeded him to Pennsylvania. He was viewed with considerable suspicion by many within the juvenile court and Department of Public Welfare. The reader must come to his own conclusions regarding the relationship between Miller's reputation and previous tactics and the juvenile court's subsequent reluctance to permit researchers access to court records. Those who are inclined to argue that access would have been permitted to a more neutral party must ask themselves why no one else had previously sought or been granted comparable access to the Pennsylvania juvenile courts. Miller's aggressive style and confrontation tactics must inevitably have contributed to the resistance and suspicion with which researchers were greeted. Without Miller's aggressiveness, however, the project might never have been undertaken. The choice may not have been between Miller and someone less objectionable to the juvenile court but between Miller and inactivity.

Officially the data collection effort was to have been the first of the monitoring and inspection programs mandated by the Federal Juvenile Justice and Delinquency Prevention Act (1974), more commonly referred to as the Bayh Act (section 223, a, 14). According to the Bayh Act, receipt of federal funds authorized under the act is contingent on a system of "on-site monitoring and inspection" of detention practices within the state. The primary thrust of the act, and presumably the thrust of monitoring and inspection, is the creation of differential detention and institutional confinement practices for criminal and status offenders. The federal agency created to execute the provisions of the Bayh Act defined *criminal offenders* as offenders charged with an offense that would be a criminal or misdemeanor offense if committed by an adult. *Status offenders* are those charged with behavior applicable only to minors: ungovernable, incorrigible, runaway, and curfew violations. *Non-offenders* are defined as those youth under the authority of the court as "deprived" or "dependent" children. The Bayh Act envisions separate treatment mechanisms for each of these three groupings. Somehow the non-offender classification was completely ignored until over halfway through the data-collection process. Even then two of the four teams were so accustomed to labeling all noncriminal detentions as status that the non-offender population remained unreported or underreported. This omission is unfortunate because it forecloses the possibility of examining another area of compliance. Although the juvenile court was under no legal obligation to distinguish between criminal and status offenders, it was obliged not to detain deprived youth with delinquent youth (section 14, 4, d). All counties studied with a juvenile detention center detained deprived and delinquent youths together, and many of the counties detained deprived youths in the county jail. Because of the oversight in the planning and training phases of the study, the incidence of such practices remains unknown. (In Erie County, where the most extensive use of the detention center for deprived youths was made, 84 of the 579 youths detained were non-offenders. Pike County detained only 16 juveniles in the county jail during 1975; 8 of the 16 were non-offenders.)

At the time of the study, Pennsylvania law treated both criminal and status offenses as instances of delinquency (Juvenile Court Act of 1972, section 2, 2 and 3). Therefore the juvenile court was under no obligation to treat criminal and status offenders differently; the federal expectation was not binding on the court except (in theory) as a condition of receipt of Bayh Act funding. Formally at least, a study to ascertain the nature of detention provided criminal and status offenders should have presented no threat to the juvenile court. The commissioner believed that the monitoring-and-inspection effort provided the only available access to information about detention practices because monitoring and inspection were required by the federal government, the juvenile court should not have been particularly threatened by an interest in the treatment received by criminal versus status offenders, and other sources of information about decision-making practices in the juvenile court were either unreliable or unavailable.

At the insistence of the commissioner of children and youth, the Governor's Justice Commission made a limited amount of funds available for a pilot monitoring-and-inspection program. Four teams of two researchers each were employed for the data-collection phase of the project. I was part of this group. Twenty-six counties were selected by the children-and-youth staff in a manner that was arbitrary but not random. I was told that four people sat around a map of the state and picked counties. Philadelphia County was excluded because "it was too big," and Allegheny and Dauphin Counties were excluded because the staff assumed that access would be denied. The omission of these three counties prohibits claims of representativeness of the data and also eliminates race as a potential analytic factor since these counties contain the state's highest concentrations of minority residents.

An official survey instrument was constructed to obtain the following information on each detention incident: name, date of birth, age, race, sex, offense and date, admission date, discharge date, to whom discharged, and remarks. Officially at least the central piece of information was the offense since that permitted classification as either criminal or status. Researchers, however, were also instructed to enter the dates of the petition, detention hearing, adjudicatory hearing, dates and nature of previous adjudications, and final disposition in the offense and remarks columns. A one-week planning and training session was held. Thereafter each team spent two to four days in each of the selected counties with a Friday debriefing session in Harrisburg to attempt to resolve problems and compare notes. In the counties names and whatever other data were available were compiled from jail and detention-center logs. Files were pulled from juvenile probation records and log information was verified and supplemented. Frequently jail and detention-center logs contained little more information than name, date admitted, and date discharged. Many times the reason for detention was listed, but the notation under that heading was often "delinquent" or "court order" (even though court orders did not exist). It was necessary to supplement case-file data with interviews with probation-office staff in every county studied to determine the nature of the alleged offense. Because information on petitions, detention hearings, adjudicatory hearings, and so forth were not formally part of the study, it was not always possible to obtain information of this nature if it was absent from the files and probation-office staff was particularly suspicious or uncooperative. Where information was missing, those answers that could be obtained from probation-office staff were accepted and reported. There is little question that this practice contributes to considerable inaccuracy in the data—an inaccuracy that has a greater impact of the formal report on monitoring and inspection than on the present study of compliance. However, the direction of the error is such that the juvenile court looks better (that is, more rather than less in compliance). If all detained youths for whom a petition had not been filled—or could not be located—were recorded as nonoffenders or as illegally detained, the results would have been far less flattering. The resolution adopted shows the court with its best foot forward. It was during these and other more informal interactions with probation-office staff that survey personnel sought to obtain more general information about the functioning of the court.

It should be noted that the Pennsylvania Department of Public Welfare had to conduct this study. The following provisions of the welfare code are relevant:

1. Article VII, Section 701, of the Public Welfare Code vests in the Department of Public Welfare the responsibility and authority to assure within the Commonwealth the availability and equitable provision of adequate child-welfare services for all children.
2. Article VII, Section 703, of the Public Welfare Code authorizes the Department of Public Welfare to make and enforce all rules and regulations necessary and appropriate to the proper establishment of the child welfare-duties and functions vested by law in the country institution districts or their successors.
3. Article IX of the Public Welfare Code authorizes the Department of Public Welfare to make and enforce rules and regulations for the visitation, examination, and inspection by the secretary and other officers or agents of the Department of all supervised institutions which includes all institutions, associations, and societies into whose care the custody of delinquent, dependent, or neglected children may be committed or detained and which receive financial assistance either directly or indirectly from the Commonwealth.
4. Article II, Section 201, of the Public Welfare Code authorizes the Department of Public Welfare to take such measures as may be necessary to render the Commonwealth eligible for available Federal funds.

Even with the relatively uncontentious nature of the official survey instrument and the cautious stance of researchers when interacting with juvenile-court personnel, and despite welfare's clear statutory authority to undertake such a study, problems of access were encountered. Three counties denied access altogether, four counties permitted access to jail and detention-center files but denied direct access to probation-office records. (Probation-office staff supplied researchers with requested information verbally—these four counties are retained in this report despite missing or falsely reported data—and one juvenile-court judge ordered all data confiscated during the second day of the study.) In addition to court-generated problems, one survey team failed, either through lack of time or motivation, to record any but the formally requested data and information on adjudicatory outcome. Because of this failing, all five counties surveyed by that team are dropped from this study. This is particularly unfortunate since three of these counties, Bucks, Chester, and Delaware, are major urban counties adjacent to Philadelphia. The analysis presented here uses the survey and interview data relevant to court compliance that was obtained from the remaining seventeen counties. Many of the observations offered in chapters 5 and 6 are based on further interviews conducted by the author with welfare officials, counsel to juveniles (in Philadelphia), staff of the Juvenile Justice Center (Philadelphia), staff of the legislature's judiciary committee, staff of the Governor's Justice Commission, and staff of the Juvenile Court Judges Commission. Most of these interviews took place during the month following the study when the author was compiling recommendations for further—and more aggressive—"monitoring and inspection" activities for the Office of Children and Youth.

Findings

The preceding description of the study design and the data-collection process is sufficient to occasion skepticism regarding the accuracy of this data. If precise measurement were required for the assessment of compliance in this instance, analysis might prove impossible with respect to several key factors. For instance, it is possible that some counties held many more detention hearings than are reported here. Detention hearings may have been held but not recorded in the case file. The case files in most counties were maintained in a manner demonstrating a clear lack of concern for procedural niceties of this type. Case files were also frequently so disorganized that researchers could have overlooked several reports of detention hearings.

Because of problems of access, problems associated with poor county record-keeping practices and—to a lesser extent—potential researcher carelessness with respect to those hidden agenda items, only very safe or general observations are offered. For instance, it is safe to argue that Northampton County has not complied with the seventy-two-hour detention-hearing expectation. Of the 501 juveniles detained, 192 were held for more than five days and 276 were held in excess of three days. Survey data indicates that only three detention hearings were held, two of which resulted in release. Only 1 of the 501 juveniles received a detention hearing according to the survey findings. One could concede (but there is no reason for such an extreme concession) that the data omitted thirty, fifty, or even more detention hearings. The conclusion that Northampton County is not in compliance with the seventy-two-hour detention-hearing provision would still stand. Similarly the discrepancies between incidence as reported by the data and legal expectations are so large that considerable inaccuracy might exist without refuting the claim that noncompliance was pervasive. At best more meticulous data might demonstrate differing levels of noncompliance among counties. Potential weaknesses aside, the data is more than sufficient to conclude that juvenile-court noncompliance with the following expectations is pervasive.

Seventy-two-Hour Detention Hearing

According to the Juvenile Court Act, "an informal detention hearing shall be held promptly by the court . . . and not later than seventy-two hours after he is placed in detention" (section 15, b). The survey, consistent with county and state recording practices, counted any part of a day as a full day's detention; that is, a youth detained at 11:00 P.M. and released the following morning at 8:00 A.M. (nine hours) is counted as having been detained two days. It is therefore necessary to count only detention incidents of five days or more as detention exceeding seventy-two hours. Table 4-1, column two, shows the numbers of juveniles detained more than three days in each county, and column three shows the number of juveniles detained more than five days. Column four provides the total number of detention hearings noted by the survey team; the number in parentheses is the number of juveniles whose detention was continued as a result of the detention hearing. For a county to be in full compliance with the seventy-two-hour detention-hearing expectation, the

Table 4-1
Detention Hearings

County	Juveniles Detained	Juveniles Detained More than 3 Days #	%	Juveniles Detained More than 5 Days #	%	Detention Hearings
Adams	67	31	(46)	8	(12)	N.A.[a]
Bradford	166	103	(62)	87	(52)	3 (1)
Cambria	316	159	(50)	103	(33)	0
Columbia	86	41	(48)	23	(27)	3 (2)
Crawford	301	109	(36)	75	(25)	[b]
Erie	579	342	(59)	241	(42)	24 (9)
Fayette	125	70	(56)	40	(32)	0
Lancaster	319	217	(68)	168	(53)	N.A.
Lebanon	108	65	(60)	45	(42)	0
Lehigh	372	242	(65)	160	(43)	[c]
Lycoming	153	67	(44)	51	(33)	5 (3)
Northampton	501	276	(55)	192	(38)	3 (1)
Northumberland	144	59	(41)	44	(31)	N.A.
Pike	16	1	(6)	1	(6)	0
Tioga	133	68	(51)	39	(30)	0
Warren	85	53	(62)	35	(41)	0
Wayne	19	7	(37)	2	(11)	N.A.
Total	3490	1910	(55)	1314	(38)	38 (16)

[a]Not available: Survey team was not permitted access to the files.
[b]Survey team made no effort to note detention hearings.
[c]The raw data for Lehigh County were misplaced.

number in the parentheses (column four) has to equal the number in column two minus whatever number of those were not actually detained for over seventy-two hours—minimally the number listed in column three. Obviously compliance in this instance is virtually nonexistent.

It is sometimes suggested that the seventy-two hour expectation—though not honored—has a moderating effect on the length of juvenile detention. However, if one notes the number of cases in column two (or three) as a percentage of all detention incidents (column one), the moderating influence is not very powerful.

Five-Day Detention in Jail

The Juvenile Court Act states that "under no circumstances shall a child be detained, placed, or committed in any facility with adults, or where he or she is apt to be abused by other children unless there is no appropriate facility available, in which case the child shall be kept separate and apart from such adults at all times and shall be detained, placed, or otherwise committed under such circumstances for not more than five days'' (section 14, 4). While all jails that housed juveniles in the counties studied attempted to segregate the adult and juvenile populations, there is considerable evidence that their efforts were less than successful. Where modest success was found, it was frequently achieved by keeping the juveniles confined in their cells for most if not all of the day. The question of compliance is difficult because the operational meaning of ''separate and apart'' can be debated. The expectation that juveniles detained in county jails with adults be so detained for not more than five days is, however, incontestably clear. Table 4-2, column three, indicates the number of juveniles detained in county jails in excess of five days. Certainly compliance demands that no juveniles be detained in jail for these periods; the only counties, however, that did not violate this expectation are those that did not detain juveniles in the jail at all.

Ten-Day Adjudicatory Hearing

The Juvenile Court Act requires that ''after the petition has been filed the court shall fix a time for hearing thereon, which, if the child

Table 4-2
Limits on Detention and Use of the County Jail

County	*Juveniles Detained*	*Juveniles Detained More than 10 Days* #	%	*Juveniles Detained More than 5 Days* #	%	*Detained in Jail in County with Detention*
Adams	67	4	(6)	1	(1.5)	7
Bradford	166	67	(40)	74	(45)	135
Cambria	316	86	(27)	0	(0)	0
Columbia	86	14	(16)	23	(27)	
Crawford	301	44	(15)	36	(12)	276
Erie	579	161	(28)	9	(1.5)	25
Fayette	125	19	(15)	40	(32)	
Lancaster	319	130	(41)	0	(0)	0
Lebanon	108	26	(24)	45	(42)	
Lehigh	372	108	(29)	64	(17)	174
Lycoming	153	30	(20)	51	(33)	
Northampton	501	123	(25)	10	(2)	25
Northumberland	144	20	(14)	44	(31)	
Pike	16	1	(6)	1	(6)	
Tioga	133	24	(18)	19	(14)	69
Warren	85	15	(18)	35	(41)	
Wayne	19	1	(5)	2	(10)	
Total	3490	873	(25)	462	(13)	711

[a]Of the juveniles detained in jail, 35 percent were held more than five days.

is in detention, shall be not later than ten days after filing of the petition'' (section 18, a). Petitions must be filed prior to or at the time of detention. Since the Juvenile Court Act makes no provision for postadjudicatory detention, any detention in excess of ten days (or less if petition has been filed prior to the initiation of detention), except as may be permissible to facilitate administrative transfer, should be considered an instance of noncompliance. Table 4-2, column two, indicates the number of juveniles detained in excess of ten days. Except for that small perentage who may legitimately be awaiting administrative transfer, these cases represent noncompliance with the expectation that either adjudicatory hearings be held within ten days or detention facilities not be used for the execution of sentence. Postadjudicatory detention would also be warranted if—following an adjudication of delinquency—the hearing were continued to permit time to study dispositional alternatives. There is no evidence, however, to suggest that any of the counties routinely separate the adjudication and disposition phases of the hearing in this manner. (In some of the counties this separation was occasionally noted.)

Detention in Jail When a Detention Center Is Available

Section 14, 4 of the Juvenile Court Act permits use of the county jail for juvenile detention only in situations in which ''there is no appropriate facility available.'' For present purposes, a detention center in an adjoining county that had available space and was willing to provide detention on a per diem basis (as they apparently all were) was not considered an ''available facility.'' Available facility refers to only those detention centers within the county in question. Space limitations in an existing county detention facility did not warrant the use of the county jail, nor were ''administrative transfers'' initiated for reasons of discipline or security accepted as warranted. If the county had a juvenile detention facility, the county jail could not be used. Table 4-2, column four, lists the number of juveniles detained in the county jail. An X in the line indicates that the county in question did not have a detention center. Only two of the counties studied did not use the county jail.

Six-Month Review and Twelve-Month Dispositional Review Hearing

The assessment of court compliance with the expectations of six-month reviews and twelve-month review hearings requires a few more assumptions than does the assessment of the other provisions. As near as I can determine, no one knows what court behavior is necessary to satisfy the six-month-review requirement. This uncertainty itself may be sufficient proof that such reviews did not take place routinely. Several members of juvenile-court staffs suggested that if the judge and the probation-office staff met to discuss an institutional commitment, such a meeting fulfilled the review expectation. The survey teams saw no indication in juvenile case files, however, that any hearings were held. Lacking evidence to the contrary, it was assumed that if dispositional review hearings were not held, six-month reviews were not held either, since the dispositional review hearing is the more substantive expectation of the two.

Were dispositional review hearings held? Since the survey covered only a twelve-month period, it was not expected that juveniles adjudicated during that period also had a review hearing in the same period. The case files were examined, however, from ten to twelve months after the end of the twelve-month period studied. This is more than sufficient time for such hearings to have been held and recorded in the case file. In addition, juveniles committed to institutions during 1974 should have returned for review hearings during 1975. If they returned, they would undoubtedly have been detained locally and would, therefore, have appeared in the survey data.

Several counties did send juveniles to the State Correctional Institution at Camp Hill (until August 1975 when it was closed to new juvenile referrals) for three months at the diagnostic and classification center. These juveniles were returned to local detention to have their commitment reviewed by the court. There exists no comparable indication that the twelve-month dispositional review hearings were held. While court personnel maintained that they constantly reviewed commitments, no one interviewed suggested that formal hearings were held; everyone outside of the court felt certain that such hearings were not held.

Impact of Gault

The Juvenile Court Act reinforces by statute many of the rights afforded juveniles in *Kent* v. *United States* and *In re Gault*. Several such provisions are listed below:

1. Except as otherwise provided in this act a party is entitled to representation by legal counsel at all stages of a

proceeding . . . and if he is without financial resources or otherwise unable to employ counsel, to have the court provide counsel for him . . . Counsel must be provided a child unless his parent, guardian, or custodian is present in court and actively waives it. However, the parent, guardian, or custodian may not waive counsel for a child when their interests may be in conflict with the interest or interests of the child. If the interest of two or more parties may conflict, separate counsel shall be provided for each of them. (section 20)

2. A party is entitled to the opportunity to introduce evidence and otherwise be heard in his own behalf and to cross-examine witnesses. (section 21, a)
3. A child charged with a delinquent act need not be a witness against or otherwise incriminate himself. . . . A confession validly made by a child out of court at a time when the child is under eighteen years of age shall be insufficient to support an adjudication of delinquency unless it is corroborated by other evidence. (section 21, b)
4. If requested by the party or ordered by the court, the proceedings shall be recorded by appropriate means. If not so recorded, full minutes of the proceedings shall be kept by the court. (section 19, c)
5. The parties or their counsel shall be afforded an opportunity to examine and controvert written reports so received and to cross-examine individuals making the reports. (section 23, d)

Provisions two through five require representation by counsel as envisioned in provision one for their proper execution. What then was the role of counsel in the juvenile courts studied? There was not one reference to counsel in any of the case files reviewed. Every member of the juvenile-court staff I interviewed was very defensive and uncooperative when discussion moved to issues such as those in provisions one through five. (While it is not possible to be certain, I was convinced that more than half of the juvenile probation officers were not aware that these provisions were actually required by the Juvenile Court Act.) The other researchers reported similar observations. The survey staff had no opportunity to directly observe the juvenile court in operation. On the basis of the juvenile-court staffs' response to questions, informed opinions of others interviewed, and what may reasonably be inferred, I am confident that neither the Supreme

Court decisions nor the provisions of the Juvenile Court Act have had an appreciable impact.

Alternative Data Sources

Both the Juvenile Court Judges Commission and the Department of Public Welfare generate a considerable amount of data relevant to the operation of the juvenile court. It would be reasonable—but incorrect—to suppose that the study of compliance undertaken would be enhanced by supplementing the data from the monitoring-and- inspection study with information from these other sources. Both Juvenile Court Judges Commission and Department of Public Welfare data, however, are useless for such purposes.

Table 4-3 presents a comparison of Juvenile Court Judges Commission detention statistics and comparable data from the monitoring-and-inspection study. Unless one is willing to assume that jail and detention-center personnel deliberately inflated records

Table 4-3
The Adequacy of Official Data

County	*# Juveniles Referred to Court: JCJC*[a]	*# Youth Detained: JCJC*	*# Youth Detained: M & I*[b]	*% Detained JCJC over % Detained M & I*
Adams	174	52	67	78
Bradford	93	22	166	13
Cambria	372	55	316	17
Columbia	66	14	86	16
Crawford	276	52	301	17
Erie	840	183	579	39
Fayette	654	55	125	44
Lancaster	714	100	319	31
Lebanon	170	39	108	36
Lehigh	492	80	372	22
Lycoming	198	83	153	54
Northampton	748	143	501	29
Northumberland	267	42	114	37
Pike	5	4	16	25
Tioga	100	39	133	29
Warren	159	49	85	58
Wayne	11	2	19	11
Total	5319	1014	3490	29

[a]JCJC: Juvenile Court Judges Commission figures.

[b]M & I: Monitoring and inspection figures.

of their population by logging in individuals who were not really detained, the monitoring-and-inspection figures can only err in the direction of underestimation. Adams County is the only county in which the number of detention incidents reported by the two sources are even modestly close. Columns two and three of table 4-3 compare the numbers of youths allegedly detained during 1975 according to the two sources. Column four provides the percentage of detention incidents reported by the Juvenile Court Judges Commission data. In only four of the seventeen counties do Juvenile Court Judges Commission data account for more than 37 percent of the detention incidents. In five of the counties more juveniles were detained than were reported as referrals to the court by Juvenile Court Judges Commission statistics (columns one and three).

There can be no question but that the Juvenile Court Judges Commission statistics, derived from data reported to the commission by the local courts, dramatically underestimate the number of detention incidents. Unless those instances reported are representative of the total population, there is no reason to trust the reliability of any of the statistics generated from this source.

The Department of Public Welfare maintains many records on the functioning of the juvenile court in connection with its funding and reimbursement responsibilities for county costs for services provided to children and youths. Such records as are kept are internal documents and are not publicly reported except in such aggregate form as renders the information unintelligible. During the course of the survey, I examined welfare records from the county courts. Most figures were reported with reference to classes of service provided and as such cannot be linked to specific juvenile cases, detention incidents, or other variables. Even so, I subsequently attempted on several occasions to obtain welfare data on county detention for 1975. It would be interesting to compare the total number of detention days each county billed to the state with the detention figures obtained from this study and as reported by Juvenile Court Judges Commission data. Thus far I have been unsuccessful in my attempts to obtain any such information from the departments.

Conclusion

The reader may be inclined to see the preceding discussions of problems of access, poor record-keeping practices, and unreliable secondary data as inelegant justifications of inadequacies in the research. I am convinced of the accuracy of the allegation of pervasive noncompliance with the legislative provisions discussed. Were better access provided, juvenile-court records to attend more adequately to legal and procedural matters, and other relevant information available, I have no doubt that the findings here would be replicated, and the discussion of noncompliance could be extended to numerous other legislative or judicial expectations presumably binding on the juvenile court.

The observation that access is difficult is perhaps the most significant explanatory observation that can be offered for the pervasiveness of juvenile-court noncompliance. The juvenile court has always been permitted—and continues to be permitted—to function in secrecy. Juvenile court behavior is invisible. It operates without oversight or external review.

5 Noncompliance and the Absence of Oversight

The extent of noncompliance of the juvenile courts with the provisions of the Juvenile Court Act precludes isolating high- and low-compliance counties from the sample and subsequently searching for variables on which these groupings might differ. Philadelphia was the only county in the state that approached technical compliance as of 1975. Philadelphia is so different from those counties studied, however, that any but the most cautious comparison is unwarranted. Those minor differences among the counties studied appear with respect to one or two isolated factors; no general patterns emerge. In those rare instances where compliance was achieved, or approached with respect to one of the expectations studied, it was more fortuitous than intentional. For instance, in one county that used the detention facility exclusively, the survey team learned that the juvenile court was very unhappy about this condition. Use of the jail was not abandoned because the juvenile court sought to comply but because the warden at the jail refused to accept juvenile referrals consequent to a misunderstanding between the jail and the juvenile probation office. In every other respect this juvenile court did no more to comply than did the courts in other counties.

Some counties detained juveniles for considerably longer periods of time than other counties. All counties, however, detained juveniles longer than seventy-two hours without a detention hearing and longer than ten days without an adjudicatory hearing. Although an argument could be made to the contrary, I do not accept shorter periods of detention as evidence of movement toward compliance. Shorter periods of detention were for reasons other than the wish to comply.

The observations in chapter 4 demonstrate the extent of noncompliance in the Pennsylvania Juvenile Court just as previous studies have documented the extent of noncompliance in other areas. Like the data from these other studies, the data in chapter 4 are insufficient to explain noncompliance. The search for explanatory hypotheses must take another course.

Chapter 3 reviewed the literature on compliance. Even though chapter 3 sought to discredit the utility of the hypotheses generated by that literature, it is necessary to consider several of them in light of the findings presented in chapter 4.

1. Several studies suggested that specificity and lack of ambiguity of decisions and/or expectations were critical to compliance. It is difficult to imagine more specific, unambiguous expectations than those examined in chapter 4. Specificity may be necessary, but it is clearly not sufficient, at least not in this context.
2. Wasby (1970) suggests that courts will be more likely to comply than other government units. The argument may be valid with respect to adult criminal and civil courts, but the author is disinclined to believe that any other public entity would be less likely to comply than did the juvenile courts in the counties studied.
3. Wasby suggests that organizations with a history of extensive discretionary power are better able to avoid compliance. Few public organizations are reputed to have more expansive discretion than the juvenile court and few public organizations could be expected to have more successfully avoided compliance. It remains to demonstrate the nature of the relationship between discretion and noncompliance.

Two additional potential explanations of noncompliance will be examined in greater detail. The first is that there exists a generalized public sentiment, a pressure, or a local value system or ethos which mitigates against compliance. This may be situationally true, but the following section will demonstrate that this assumption has gained currency primarily as a result of the unrepresentative nature of the selection process operative in compliance research. A second section will explore the possibility that strong vested interests or preferences within the juvenile court may make it organizationally significant that compliance be avoided. It will be asserted that, at least over the predictable short run, there are no logically compelling reasons which are sufficient to explain noncompliance of the magnitude in chapter 4. The assumption presented in the final and major section of this chapter asserts that while there may have been no clear utility to be gained through noncompliance, there was even less reason to comply. This section focuses on the absence or abdication of any enforcement, regulatory, or oversight responsibility with respect to juvenile court behavior.

Public Consequences of Compliance

The Supreme Court's decision in *Brown* v. *Board of Education* struck at the very heart of social and institutional values in American society. If racial segregation was not permitted in the public schools, racial segregation obviously would be prohibited in other arenas. The heated public debates, angry crowds, and national-guard troops attest to the intense public hostility to desegregation. It has been suggested that white flight from urban areas was intensified and private and parochial schools revitalized as a direct consequence of desegregation. This argument may be overstated and oversimplified, but its general relevance is irrefutable. In attacking segregation in the public schools, the Supreme Court demanded that locally elected public officials, whatever their personal sentiments, take action destined to generate public hostility and conflict. In such circumstances noncompliance of public officials may be disappointing, but it is hardly surprising.

Because *Brown* v. *Board of Education* spoke to such politically and socially sensitive issues and because these issues—at least symbolically—were presumed to have universal and potentially profound consequences for American society, it is unfortunate that the initial studies of compliance dealt with this decision so frequently. Although it was neither as visible nor as potentially significant, the *Schempp* decision regarding devotional exercises in the public schools raised an issue that is also emotionally and ideologically volatile. Public sentiment and response to issues of this nature are likely to exert an influence on offical compliance. Issues like this, however, are the exception rather than the rule.

Public reaction and media attention to school desegregation in Boston was extensive. Just previous to the decision, however, all of the state's juvenile institutions were closed. Massive public demonstrations were not mounted nor were returning juveniles attacked with American flags. This is not to suggest that public support for deinstitutionalization exceeded support for desegregation in Massachusetts; in fact, it is likely that a public referendum would find that desegregation was more widely supported. However, those who oppose deinstitutionalization do so with markedly less intensity than do those who oppose desegregation. Within juvenile justice and academic circles, deinstitutionalization is regarded as the most controversial issue since the creation of the juvenile court. At best the general public is passively hostile. It is likely that the majority of residents of Massachusetts did not know and still do not know that juvenile deinstitutionalization occurred in their state. And virtually none outside of the state knows that it happened. (Interviews conducted in 1975, 1976, and 1977 with Pennsylvania juvenile-court probation officers indicated that the majority of even this group knew little or nothing about deinstitutionalization in Massachusetts.) If a change of this magnitude can occur without extensive public involvement, it is unlikely that public opinion would be a meaningful factor associated with court compliance with either *Gault* or the provisions of the Pennsylvania Juvenile Court Act.

Unfortunately many of the hypotheses generated in the compliance literature anticipated the clash of intensely held social, political, and ideological values in the decision to comply or not to comply. It is reasonable to assume that for locally elected officials to have willingly complied with *Brown* might have meant political suicide. It may be unduly romantic to characterize official compliance with *Brown* as an heroic act, but it would be naive to suggest that there were not attendant risks in the larger social, political environment. In the virtually invisible world of juvenile justice, however, it is impossible to imagine a general public outcry because judges permit juveniles the right to counsel, that cross-examination of witnesses is permitted, detention hearings are held within seventy-two hours, detained juveniles are afforded adjudicatory hearings within ten days, juveniles detained in jail are afforded adjudicatory hearings within five days, counties with juvenile detention facilities do not also use the local jail for juvenile detention, or deprived children are not placed in the same facilities with delinquent children. There is no generalized public support for either the expectations of *Gault* or the provisions of the Juvenile Court Act, however, it is likely that if the public considered these matters at all, they would take them to be essentially unnecessary administrative niceties. Neither the absence nor the presence of such practices in the juvenile court would be sufficient to arouse public concern.

Noncompliance with *Brown* v. *Board of Education* may well have been determined in large part by strongly held and aggressively articulated public sentiment. While allegations positing strong public sentiment either for or against compliance with most legislatively or judicially imposed expectations are used by officals to rationalize their behavior, there is every reason to believe that *Brown* v. *Board of Education* is atypical in this respect. It appears that compliance or noncompliance with the provisions of the Juvenile Court Act and the majority of essentially administrative expectations imposed on public officials is not influenced greatly by public sentiment.

It might be conceded that there is no significant concern with how the juvenile court functions internally. The public does demand certain output criteria, however. These expectations may be no more ambitious than that the court restrain the behavior and freedom of certain types of juveniles in certain situations. The local police are far more likely to receive criticism than is the court when juvenile misconduct exceeds the level a community is willing to tolerate. It is possible, for instance, that the juvenile court—including juvenile probation—could cease to exist in the counties studied without anyone noticing. This of course presumes that the demise of the court could be kept secret. It is unnecessary and unprofitable, therefore, to posit a relationship between generalized public and political sentiment and compliance with the essentially administrative, procedural provisions of the Juvenile Court Act. Juvenile-court staff frequently alleged that the public demanded behavior inconsistent with legally imposed obligations of the court. The public here, as elsewhere, exists as an organizational myth serving to justify official conduct. The public in this sense is an interesting fictional creation, but its utility in explaining juvenile-court behavior cannot be underestimated. Although a modest and short-lived public clamor can be orchestrated around specific cases or issues from time to time, public sentiment is an insufficient explanation of most instances of noncompliance.

Consequences for the Court

As of 1975 compliance with the provisions of the Pennsylvania Juvenile Court Act was minimal in the counties studied. Philadelphia County was the only county in the state that approached technical compliance at that time. I have heard unsubstantiated claims that other counties subsequently adopted policies that move in the direction of compliance. The effective date of the Juvenile Court Act was January 1973; the study reported here was conducted in November and December of 1976 and January of 1977. The data on detention practices reflect court practices two to three years after the legislation became effective. Interview data refers to a state of affairs four years after the effective date. Several apologists for the court have suggested that change takes time and it may still be premature to accuse the court of culpable noncompliance. Others have suggested that programmatic obstacles to compliance exist. One chief probation officer noted that it would be impossible to satisfy the statutory expectations regarding detention and adjudicatory hearings in his county since juvenile court was only held once a month. He was singularly unimpressed by the suggestion that it could be held more frequently if the law so required. A minority suggested that the statutory provisions in question were either unnecessary or inappropriate. While these observations may have merit in their own right, they are uncharacteristic coming from juvenile-court personnel who, in other situations, are so comfortable explaining to juveniles, particularly status offenders, that the law must be obeyed because it is the law. One juvenile-court judge observed with unusual candor that he had no intention of recognizing certain elements of the statutory provisions because such provisions were motivated solely by an irresponsible desire to save money—a saving, as he saw it, at the expense of the best interests of the juveniles. And although a specific account of juvenile-court practice in his county is impossible (the judge confiscated all data during the second day of the site visit under threat of arrest were all materials not turned over), the data-collection process made it clear to the survey team that the judge did seek to advance the best interests of those under his jurisdiction without the slightest regard for formally imposed expectations.

In a more typical interview, a staff member of a probation office showed great pride in that, as of 1977, his office had established a firm policy of holding detention hearings within ten days (seventy-two-hour statutory expectation) and adjudicatory hearings for detained juveniles within twenty-five days (ten-day statutory expectations). That such a minor movement toward compliance should occasion apparently genuine professional pride is the most telling information that may be gained from the interview data. (I suggest that there are those who find such a policy substantially inadequate. Not only would such an observation have brought the interview abruptly to a close, but, more significantly, there appeared to be no possibility that the subject could appreciate such a literal, legalistic interpretation of legislative intent. This disregard for the formal expectation of the Juvenile Court Act was representative of most juvenile court personnel interviewed.)

Given the pervasiveness of noncompliance, one might suspect that the Juvenile Court Act posed a significant threat to the functioning of the juvenile court. Surely the courts would not, en masse, disregard the law unless some substantial interest was at stake. The search for such a compelling interest, however, is problematic without adapting a long-range speculative perspective. The Juvenile Court Act requires two new hearings and one review. At best, over the short run, there is nothing in the legislation that would compel the court to change its current decision-making practices. Beyond requiring that such hearings and reviews be held, the legislation imposed no substantive, specific criteria for such occasions. There is nothing to preclude perfunctory, ritualistic hearings that formally justify whatever juvenile-court practice is currently desired.

Over the long run, however, such hearings may lead to change. The Juvenile Court Act does extend the right to counsel to all juvenile hearings. Counsel at such hearings might argue, as has been done successfully with regard to legislative provisions elsewhere, that the legislature must have intended that a hearing serve some more legitimate purpose than to sanctify those decisions previously determined informally. If counsel became actively involved in the juvenile court and such hearings were held, it might be only a matter of time until procedural and substantive questions about these hearings and reviews were advanced on appeal. As of 1978, however, it was unclear whether or not the juvenile must be present at these hearings or what criteria are sufficient to warrant continued confinement. The 1977 amendments to the Juvenile Court Act requires a "probable cause" determination for juveniles detained for "delinquent" offenses. Otherwise detention is permissible if, in the court's judgment, such detention "is required to protect the person or property of others or of the child or because the child may abscond, or be removed from the jurisdiction of the court or because he has no parent, guardian, or custodian or other person able to provide supervision and care for him or an order for his detention or shelter care has been made by the court pursuant to this act."

If the court has a vested interest that is being protected by noncompliance with the hearing and review requirements, it must be an interest that will be sacrificed to some future appellate-court ruling with regard to criteria for, and outcome of, these proceedings. However, the court is only required to inconvenience itself by holding a hearing, the form of which remains completely undefined. Obviously, the expectation that adjudicatory hearings be held within ten days for detained juveniles—five days for juveniles detained in jail—

demands no more than that the court inconvenience itself somewhat with respect to scheduling. If Philadelphia County, which according to Juvenile Court Judges Commission figures processed 42.3 percent of all the juvenile-court cases in the state in 1975, can meet this expectation, it is difficult to understand why other courts cannot meet the expectation with some frequency. Except where the court may wish, for whatever reason, to detain a juvenile for up to or more than ten days without any intention of formally hearing the case, it is difficult to identify any short-term interest that is protected through noncompliance other than scheduling convenience.

The other expectations of the Juvenile Court Act examined here pertain to the definition of appropriate detention facilities. A portion of the costs of constructing juvenile facilities are currently a county responsibility. Many rural courts have argued that their respective counties are unwilling to undertake the cost of such construction, nor are they willing to incur the costs of transferring juveniles to detention facilities in adjoining counties. Again this is an instance of prescriptive legislation being treated as though it were merely enabling. The 1977 amendments to the Juvenile Court Act anticipated local noncompliance by requiring the Department of Public Welfare to construct mandated facilities and bill the counties if compliance was not obtained by a certain date. In reference to the 1973 legislation, juvenile-court personnel were incredulous at the suggestion that if counties were unwilling to provide the legislatively mandated facilities, the law could be observed by abstaining from detaining juveniles.

It certainly would be preposterous for an individual to seek to excuse himself from the expectations of law because he is unwilling to incur the expense necessary for compliance. While it may be appropriate to formally appeal the propriety of an expectation that imposes financial hardship, it is an altogether different matter to assume that one's casual assertion of hardship is sufficient to justify noncompliance. I have been unable to identify any instance on which the juvenile court has formally argued against the appropriateness of any of the statutory provisions discussed in this book. Surely juvenile-court judges individually or collectively, through the Juvenile Court Judges Commission, have easy access to all relevant legislative committees should they wish to object to the unreasonableness or impropriety of any of the legislative provisions. Nowhere in the literature of the Juvenile Court Judges Commission is there a hint that any of these expectations are the least bit contentious, nor is there the suggestion that they may be routinely and flagrantly violated by the court.

If the preceding argument is convincing, it is difficult to determine what the court gains through noncompliance. It is sufficient to ask what the court risks by noncompliance. It is inevitable that noncompliance would be seen as a consequence of fervent ideological commitment to the tenets of traditional juvenile-court philosophy. This explanation is particularly attractive when applied to the particular judge who alleged that most current efforts at juvenile-court reform were motivated by an uncaring legislative and administrative concern for cost reduction. Such an argument is ultimately unacceptable. Programmatically it is unacceptable because it explains very little; prescriptively it is unacceptable because, were it valid, nothing could be done to change it; and empirically it is unacceptable because contact with various Pennsylvania juvenile courts provides no basis for positing the existence of a uniform juvenile-court philosophy, ideology, or style to explain the consistent noncompliance.

This is not an attempt to refute the Stapleton and Teitlebaum (1973) hypothesis that veteran juvenile-court judges are less likely to comply than those who are newer to the bench. In fact, interviews with two juvenile-court judges who took the bench after 1975 suggest that both intended to initiate changes that anticipate compliance with selected provisions of the Juvenile Court Act. One initiated a *Miranda*-like procedure more aggressive than anything as yet suggested as necessary by appellate courts. It is inevitable that new people in any organization more readily adopt those expectations in place at the time of their arrival than do those with considerable experience under an older system. Beyond this, however, the ideological-commitment hypothesis has little to recommend it. In addition, unless differential levels of ideological commitment can be measured apart from actual court behavior and correlated with differing levels of compliance, the hypothesis comes dangerously close to being tautological. If one merely wishes to assert that judges who do things in the old way are more ideologically committed to the old way than are those who do not, there can be no cause to quarrel with such a definition. The theoretical utility of such an assertion, however, is suspect. Hypotheses pertaining to other than personal and ideological characteristics of judges are potentially more fruitful.

The reader who remains attracted by the personal-ideology hypothesis is asked whether juvenile-court judges could be more ideologically opposed to the provisions of the Juvenile Court Act discussed here than the police were to the expectations of *Miranda*. Technical compliance with *Miranda* was prompt and pervasive—questions of impact and substantial compliance notwithstanding. Except where compliance would require behavior or outcome that the subject was unable to effect, the study of compliance is only interesting if some sentiment or motive for noncompliance exists. The questions then become under what circumstances are those who would prefer not to comply induced to do so, and what modification of circumstances might reasonably be expected to secure (at least technical) compliance.

Explaining Noncompliance

Neither county-specific nor judge-specific characteristics are a plausible explanation for the pervasive noncompliance observed in the juvenile court. The compliance literature has consistently identified the unambiguous specification of expectations as a principal factor associated with compliance. It is difficult to imagine a court decision, a statutory provision, or an administrative ruling less susceptible to criticism for ambiguity than the Juvenile Court Act; yet juvenile-court compliance is virtually nonexistent. It is possible that powerful public pressures or the desire to protect some essential institutional maintenance function can explain noncompliance. Although hypotheses of this nature are compelling in other areas in which compliance has been studied—particularly regarding school desegregation—they are unsatisfactory in the present context. How then is noncompliance to be explained?

Implicit in the reasoning of all compliance studies I have reviewed is the assumption that compliance would be routinely achieved in the absence of powerful forces mitigating against it. In these studies the attitudes and values of those of whom compliance is sought are taken to be one such force. The inadequacy of such a perspective has been noted. The analysis that follows rests on an assumption that is substantially different from those that underlie previous studies of discretion. Here attention is focused not on factors prompting noncompliance but on the absence of factors prompting compliance. If the discussion is limited to technical compliance, it is easily established that compliance is frequently achieved in the face of extensive objections from those who must comply. Technical compliance with *Miranda* is the clearest example of such unwilling, reluctant compliance. Inherent in this argument is the assumption that noncompliance might be observed even in situations in which most decision makers were neutral or mildly supportive (at least in principle) of the expectations imposed. Each reader can draw from his own experience numerous rules which are objected to by no one, but which nonetheless go unobserved. Compliance and noncompliance are ultimately determined by the interplay of factors that motivate noncompliance and induce compliance. Because previous studies have disproportionately if not exclusively attended to motives for noncompliance and the present example of juvenile-court noncompliance is particularly amenable to this type of analysis, the juvenile-court noncompliance can be explained as a consequence of the absence of inducement to comply, that is, formal or informal enforcement.

Subject-Generated Enforcement

Jowell's study (1975) of the impact of decisional review mechanisms in several public agencies in Boston suggests that the most significant factor associated with effective review is the private—individual or collective—resources that may be brought to bear to effect or enforce compliance. Davis (1969) heralds the success of administrative rulemaking prompted by the Federal Procedures Act in federal regulatory agencies. He proposes this as a model for the reduction of discretion in other public arenas. He fails, however, to consider the substantial resources—access to counsel, personal credibility and status, and political capital—at the disposal of subjects of regulatory-agency discretion. It is hardly surprising that these subjects were both willing and able to protect their interests against the legally inappropriate decisions of public officials. It is unlikely that federal regulatory agencies had, previous to the Administrative Procedures Act, offensively abused their discretionary authority by taking action against the interests of the corporate entities they were empowered to regulate. A more frequently heard, and apparently more appropriate, criticism of federal regulatory agencies is that they function to serve and protect rather than regulate the legally questionable behavior of their subjects. Davis fails to demonstrate that the discretion of regulatory officials not to regulate and control the behavior of corporate entities has been reduced by the administrative rulemaking to which he refers so approvingly. If his argument rests on the success with which subjects of regulatory agencies are protected against the unwarranted discretion of regulatory officials, there is no reason to believe, as he suggests, that such protections are transferrable to human-service organizations. In the successful examples offered by both Jowell and Davis, enforcement is a consequence of the resources at the disposal of the subjects of official discretion. In these instances enforcement must be seen as the responsibility of affected parties. Surely the subjects of juvenile-court decisions are without the necessary resources to motivate or enforce compliance. Had *Gault* occasioned the adversarial reform envisioned by most legal commentators, legal counsel may have become the resource through which compliance could be obtained. It is now clear, however, that the juvenile-court revolution anticipated in law-journal articles and juvenile-justice texts has yet to occur. The absence of effective counsel or any alternative personal resource has meant that the subject of juvenile-court decision making has been powerless to demand compliance.

Counsel in the Juvenile Court

In 1975 Philadelphia County Juvenile Court appeared to be in technical compliance with most of the formal provisions of the Juvenile Court Act. While six-month and twelve-month review hearings were frequently held in Philadelphia according to respondents, court practice was believed to fall substantially short of compliance with this provision. It is significant that Philadelphia County has had an aggressive and lengthy history of defense-counsel involvement in the juvenile court. In fact the Philadelphia County Public Defender's Office has had a separate juvenile-court unit for some time. Counsel was rarely present in the counties studied. Assumptions about causality are difficult because the same factors that prompted a general compliance with *Gault* in Philadelphia County may have also prompted compliance with the provisions of the Juvenile Court Act. It is likely, however, that the presence of counsel contributed greatly to compliance with the provisions of the Juvenile Court Act if only because objections and appeals stemming from violations of statutory provisions would have been more inconvenient than the inconvenience associated with compliance. It is easier to hold a detention hearing and retain a juvenile in detention than it is to respond to formal defense-counsel maneuvering. This is particularly true since there is currently no definition of the procedural or substantive content of such proceedings. One might not necessarily expect counsel to be particularly successful at obtaining a juvenile's release from detention, but counsel could force a hearing to take place, even if the hearing were unsubstantive.

There is reason to believe that the presence and aggressiveness of counsel would significantly reduce the level of noncompliance. Compliance would not necessarily result in any difference in disposition, that is, what some might call substantial compliance or impact. Stapleton and Teitlebaum (1973) and Canon and Kolson (1971) suggest that counsel may, at least in some jurisdictions, reduce rather than increase the juvenile's chances of securing a lenient disposition of his case. Although the interests of compliance might be served well by the presence of counsel, it is not clear that the individual juvenile's interest would be served. Obviously risks for the individual defendant would be particularly high at the initial stages in which lawyers were only beginning to practice in the juvenile court.

Why are lawyers relatively absent from the juvenile courts of the counties studied? Representing a client in a situation in which a lawyer believes such representation jeopardizes rather than advances a client's interest presents ethical problems. Forcing the court to hold a detention hearing within seventy-two hours, hold an adjudicatory hearing within ten days if his client is detained, and detain a client in a detention center rather than the county jail is a questionable victory if the lawyer and his client have reason to believe that the fruits of these successes may be that the client is committed to a juvenile institution rather than placed on probation. Consider the case of a county that frequently engaged in the practice of sentencing juveniles to weekend terms in the county jail (usually for four to twenty-six weekends). Such a practice could be successfully challenged on appeal. As the judge in one county explained to me, however, and as he would undoubtedly explain to counsel, the court had the right to commit the juveniles in question to a state youth-development center for an indefinite period. The judge asserted that if his decision were in error, it erred in the direction of excessive leniency. Were an objection to his practice of sentencing juveniles to weekend detention filed, he suggested that he would regrettably be forced to commit those juveniles to institutions. He made no acknowledgment of the possibility that the alternative to weekend detention might be probation. Given this type of intimidation and the court's authority to carry out its threat, it would appear to be ethically impossible for a lawyer to object to his client's sentence to weekend detention. Given the court's extensive legitimate authority, behavior by the juvenile or his counsel that offends the court's sense of propriety is dangerous. In Philadelphia County interviews with lawyers who regularly practice in the juvenile court reveal the belief that a cautious, nonadvisorial style is required. Current opinion among lawyers in the juvenile court is that, at best, they are social-work advocates negotiating for alternative, less punitive dispositions for their clients and rarely playing more than a negligible role in the adjudication process.

A final word about the lawyer's role in juvenile court is necessary. In adult criminal court the appeal process, although it is envoked in no more than 1 percent of cases, stands as a safeguard against at least certain types of judicial capriciousness. Appellate courts have been very reluctant to assume any supervisory responsibility with respect to the juvenile court. For example, the Juvenile Law Center of Philadelphia has on several occasions sought a writ of prohibition against a county court (other than Philadelphia) for detaining juveniles in excess of seventy-two hours without a detention hearing. In each instance the reviewing court delayed action until such time as the juvenile was released then declared the issue moot. It is alleged that informal telephone conversations between the court and the juvenile-court judge were used to facilitate this finding. Without the active protection of the appellate courts, it is unlikely that the role of counsel in juvenile courts will be perceived by the legal profession as either functional or attractive.

If, for altogether different reasons, counsel was aggressively present in the juvenile court, there is reason to believe that compliance would be substantially higher than where counsel was absent—at least with respect to procedurally specific issues. If accurate, this hypothesis would have a clear predictive utility. Given the numerous problems associated with the introduction, role, and dispositional utility of counsel, however, the hypothesis is not very exciting prescriptively. The long-range interest of juvenile reform and individual interest of future defendants in the juvenile court may be served by strategies that seek to insinuate counsel into today's juvenile court, but it is doubtful that immediate client interests are served. As a strategy for obtaining more than technical compliance, the introduction of counsel may leave a lot to be desired.

Oversight Authority

The subjects of juvenile-court decision making are without the necessary resources to inconvenience, embarrass, coerce, or otherwise motivate court compliance. Although the presence of counsel might be such a resource, for other reasons it is unlikely that counsel will play a significant role in the nonurban juvenile court for some time. What other enforcement mechanisms might be expected to impinge on the court's motivation to comply? Three such sources of pressure are obvious: legislative oversight committees (especially the Judiciary Committee), the Juvenile Court Judges Commission, and the Department of Public Welfare. Current scholarly opinion suggests that legislative oversight is rarely developed to the point where it might have an effect on behavior and compliance (Jones 1977). The staff of the legislature's Judiciary Committee was questioned with respect to the committee's oversight activity. Those interviewed were of the opinion that the committee had abdicated any oversight authority and responsibility it possessed with reference to the juvenile court. While they thought that the committee should use its legislative and particularly its funding authority to coerce juvenile-court compliance, it was thought unlikely that the committee would take such action. There is currently no cause to assume that legislative oversight provides any impetus toward compliance.

Advocates of administrative rule-making as a strategy for reducing discretion are likely to see the Juvenile Court Judges Commission as the vehicle most likely to induce court compliance. The more skeptical observer, however, is disinclined to believe that professional organizations will take a particularly aggressive role in enforcing standards on their membership. It seems more reasonable to assume that professional organizations will serve an essentially public-relations, boundary-protection function calculated to shield members from external criticism and control. To the extent that this is the central—though latent—goal sought by such professional associations, organizational effort is directed toward obtaining control of those factors associated with assessment of membership behavior and effectiveness. The cant of professionalism serves to disqualify all but group members from commenting on the appropriateness of membership conduct. This is the role the Juvenile Court Judges Commission assumed, thus foreclosing, at least presently, the possibility that the commission will play a role in enforcing compliance.

The particular strategy employed by the Juvenile Court Judges Commission to protect its membership may not be commendable, but it is efficient and informative. The commission has obtained control of virtually all resources available for data collection and study of juvenile-court functioning in Pennsylvania. All official statistics on the state's juvenile courts are generated by the Juvenile Court Judges Commission. The gross inaccuracy of such statistics is documented in chapter 4. Even if the data were meticulously accurate, however, it is neither reported nor collected in a manner that permits assessment of juvenile-court compliance. The commission collects no data on detention hearings, timing of adjudicatory hearings, or commitment-review hearings. It collects data on length of detention but does not report it. The commission's annual reports (Pennsylvania Juvenile Court Dispositions) are structured in a manner calculated to avoid controversy. Those who wish to use the reports to question or attack juvenile-court practices would have a feeble ally in the commission's data.

The Juvenile Court Judges Commission could use its authority, access to local juvenile-court records, and public-reporting responsibility to bring considerable pressure on local courts. Not surprisingly the commission employs these resources to protect the local courts. The commission is in a position to be a powerful enforcement mechanism. There is no justification, however, for presuming that it will either volunteer or be coaxed or coerced into assuming that role in the near future.

In Pennsylvania, as elsewhere, the juvenile court is a local responsibility. Most of the court's resources for handling juveniles, however, are either provided directly or funded by the state Department of Public Welfare. The control of these funds, plus the particulars of the Pennsylvania Public Welfare Code, are more than sufficient to permit the Department of Public Welfare to assume regulatory, enforcement power over local court behavior. I would argue that the welfare code mandates such a role. Whatever its role might have been or should have been, it can be asserted irrefutably that the Department of Public Welfare has consistently behaved as though its sole function with respect to juvenile justice was to serve the wishes of the juvenile court. Two examples of Department of Public Welfare behavior establish that the department has opted to be more of a coconspirator with the juvenile court than a regulatory body.

The Department of Public Welfare reimburses counties for the expense of juvenile detention. Prior to 1973 any incidence of detention was eligible for reimbursement since juvenile courts have unfettered discretion pertaining to detention. With the 1973 Juvenile Court Act certain detention practices became illegal. The Department of Public Welfare was not obliged or even permitted to pay for the illegal confinement of juveniles. Surely if the criteria for receipt of public assistance were adjusted downward by statute, the department would neither presume nor be permitted to continue to pay previously eligible but now ineligible welfare recipients.

The Department of Public Welfare has, however, continued to pay for all instances of local detention. The department had the right and responsibility to refuse payment for all statutorily prohibited instances of detention. For the same reasons, the department could and should have refused to confine or pay for the confinement of juveniles beyond twelve months unless statutorily mandated review hearings were held. Had it taken this position, the juvenile-court judges may have been unhappy and may even have had the resources to retaliate informally; but they would have had no justifiable basis for opposing or contesting the department's action. (When I suggested this strategy to the welfare-department officials who professed opposition to court practices, it was initially received as a joke. Apparently the department's role as a regulatory agency for the juvenile court was such an alien image for them that the suggestion could only be seen as playful. When the seriousness of the suggestion was affirmed, they visibly lost interest in the discussion, not because they wished to support the court but because they could not imagine opposing it.) By continuing to provide funds for illegal juvenile-court practices, the Department of Public Welfare provided a cloak of legitimacy for noncompliance.

The second example deals less directly with compliance but more directly with impact. The 1976 amendments to the Juvenile Court Act changed state reimbursement practice from one that financially rewarded counties for institutionalizing juveniles to one that was clearly intended to reward noninstitutional dispositions. The amendment specifically referred to this latter category as community-based programs. The department's response was to define many state and private institutions as "community-based programs." Apparently nothing but the label was changed. By this linguisitic maneuvering, the Department of Public Welfare permitted the juvenile court to continue to place juveniles in institutions without incurring the fiscal disincentive envisioned by the legislation. (It is only fair to note that the Department of Public Welfare operates all state juvenile institutions and consequently the department's behavior may have been motivated more by a desire to protect its own interest than to assist the juvenile court.)

It is not surprising that the Juvenile Court Judges Commission does not take a regulatory or critical stance with respect to the behavior of its own membership. Conventional wisdom (and much of traditional, prescriptive political-science and public-administration literature) suggests that the Department of Public Welfare both would and should assume that role. While it is not clear why they have not done so, it is clear that they have not. It is sufficient to maintain that the pervasive juvenile-court noncompliance would have been unlikely, if not impossible, had not the Department of Public Welfare abdicated responsibility in this area.

Juvenile Court Secrecy: A General Protection against Oversight

In addition to the official, formal sources of oversight activity, there are also numerous, less formal sources of influence, control, criticism, or review of the activities of a public organization. The media, special-interest groups, academic research or evaluation activities all represent potential sources of oversight or monitoring influence. No component of the criminal justice system except the jury is better able to protect its interests or shield its activities from external scrutiny, however, than is the juvenile court. While "confidentiality" in the juvenile court has long been cherished because of the protection it ostensibly provides the juvenile, there is every reason to believe that the principle of confidentiality is infinitely more functional as a device for protecting the court. The research reported in chapter 4 was conducted consistent with the requirements of the federal Juvenile Justice and Delinquency Prevention Act (1974) by the Department of Public Welfare, which has sufficient statutory authority (through the Pennsylvania Welfare Code) to undertake such activity. Yet six of nineteen counties refused researchers access to juvenile-court files, one juvenile-court judge confiscated the survey data, and three other counties denied access altogether. How this might protect juveniles is unclear; that it protects the juvenile court is obvious. Historically at least, the juvenile court has been able to deny access to anyone under the cover of the confidentiality argument. External oversight of any sort is unlikely as long as such self-serving practices are permitted.

Most of the observations provided thus far are not particularly surprising. That the juvenile court would be able to keep others from learning about its activities might have been expected. What is surprising is that the juvenile court itself could not discover, with any degree of accuracy, what it had done—on the unlikely assumption that it might wish to do so. Presumably the Lehigh County Juvenile Court knew that it was underreporting when it reported seventy-two detention instances in 1974 to the Juvenile Court Judges Commission (1974 data were used because they could not locate detention records for 1975). It could not have determined from its own records, however, that at least 372 juveniles had been detained that year. In every county studied, juvenile-court records failed to show some instances of detention. The reason for the detention was rarely clear. Frequently researchers were forced to assume that detention was based on a petition that had been filed more than a month before the detention incident. Many times the juvenile-court staff were unable to recall or reconstruct from the records why a juvenile was detained. Discrepancies of up to one month existed between jail or detention-center logs and juvenile-court records with respect to the length of a juvenile's detention. At least one case file contained a two- or three-page entry dated during a period when a youth was in detention without any reference anywhere to the fact that he was so detained. I never saw an indication in a case file that a petition had been dismissed for lack of proof (although the Juvenile Court Judges Commission data indicate that between 0 and 12 percent of all cases are dismissed for this reason).

As often as not, it was impossible to determine what the court's response had been to a particular petition. In several instances a juvenile had been detained, apparently adjudicated, and committed to an institution without any record of a petition having been filed. Juveniles from out-of-county or out-of-state were routinely detained without any record maintained in the juvenile probation office. There are many examples of this nature. However, individual case files were frequently voluminous. They were usually overflowing with social-work, quasi-clinical entries. What was conspicuously absent were references to legally, procedurally relevant factors.

The preceding observations are sufficient to warrant two observations. First, the social-work, antilegal bias of juvenile-court records frustrates the possibility of careful oversight even if access could be obtained. Second, the nature of record-keeping practices reveals the contempt of the juvenile court for procudural, legal expectations and the court's tacit assumption that it is exempt from any expectation that it be accountable to external review.

Other public organizations maintain very poor records. Although these records may be suspect in numerous respects, most record-keeping practices can be seen as an attempt to justify the legitimacy of organizational practices—at least to make it appear that the organization is operating within appropriate constraints. Implicit in the self-protecting nature of such record-keeping practice is an acknowledgment that extraorganizational actors have legitimate oversight rights with respect to the organization's activities. Even if the organization is unwilling to operate legitimately, it feels constrained to appear to be doing so. That the juvenile court does not even bother to keep records in a manner calculated to make the court's decision making appear legitimate is adequate proof that the court feels accountantable to no one. The court would only behave in such a manner if there were no oversight and no source of enforcement authority. Not only is the court not motivated to comply, it is not even motivated to pretend that is complies.

6 Conclusion

The principal purpose of this book was to explore the relationship between discretion and compliance and examine the utility of various hypotheses for the control of discretion and facilitation of compliance. Attention to the specifics of discretion and compliance in the Pennsylvania Juvenile Court was, in a sense, a secondary interest. Before proceeding to more general concluding remarks, however, some further observations regarding the prospects for reduced discretion and increased compliance in the court are necessary. The provisions of the Juvenile Court Act discussed here are understood as an effort to reduce the discretion of the juvenile court; minimally, these provisions formally set more restrictive limits on the court's discretionary authority. Several hypothetical circumstances in which the court's discretionary power might be reduced to the level of its statutory authority follow. At least in these instances, compliance and reduced discretion are nearly synonymous.

The Future of Discretion and Noncompliance in the Pennsylvania Juvenile Court

The activist reader, anxious to reform the juvenile court, may be impatient with the discussion that has thus far avoided consideration of substantial compliance or impact. It is not reasonable to ask why anyone should be interested in technical compliance if it is clear that technical compliance can be obtained without impact and without providing any necessary motivation to substantial compliance. It is just as reasonable to ask how legislative, judicial, or administrative efforts to secure the major transformations in court behavior will succeed if such efforts are not even sufficient to induce an essentially nonthreatening technical compliance. For instance, if detention hearings are to have any opportunity to have an impact on the detention decision, they must first be held. If held, decisions in such hearings become subject to formal review, become more formally visible, and make at least modest progress toward making previously secret policy public. It is obvious that juvenile-court decision-making practices regarding detention will not necessarily change because detention hearings are held. Detention hearings do not guarantee change, but they do provide an opportunity for change to occur. An examination of technical compliance is an essential first step in understanding the dynamics of compliance with the Juvenile Court Act and the nature of the discretion the juvenile court possesses. Except under unusual circumstances, it is fruitless to try to understand impact unless a change has occurred.

It was suggested that those with an interest in motivating compliance are without the necessary resources to do so. Those with potentially sufficient resources and responsibility to enforce compliance have made no effort to do so. The appellate courts, Department of Public Welfare, and Juvenile Court Judges Commission have been accused of assisting or permitting noncompliance with the provisions of the Juvenile Court Act. Must it be assumed that the absence of externally imposed inducements to comply will continue unaltered into the forseeable future? If so, there is no reason to believe that juvenile-court compliance is likely. If not, what form are future pressures to comply likely to take?

There is growing dissatisfaction with the functioning of the juvenile court. The short-term consequences of the Supreme Court decisions in *Kent, Gault*, and *Winship* and the subsequent revisions in most jurisdictions of state juvenile codes may have taken the immediate pressure off the court. There is doubt that there was an assumption that these formal legal changes would produce operational change. The secrecy in which the juvenile court functions has been a major impediment to the correction of this false assumption. Those who now wish to question the appropriateness of court functioning, however, can add juvenile-court lawlessness to the already substantial list of criticisms. The widespread acknowledgment that a court—even the juvenile court—flagrantly and willfully disregards the law may ultimately become a source of embarrassment. Whether widespread attention will focus on juvenile-court noncompliance and whether that attention will be sufficient to induce the level of embarrassment required to motivate at least token compliance is uncertain.

It is even possible, though unlikely, that the court's open disregard for the formal expectations of the law will precipitate more significant change and more dramatic reduction of the court's discretionary authority and power than anything envisioned in the provisions of the Juvenile Court Act. The court's contempt for formal authority may ultimately offend those who were relatively unmoved by the court's disregard for the rights of and the treatment received by its charges. Since it is unclear how the juvenile court came to have the rather considerable informal influence with elected, appointed, and civil-service officials that it appears to possess, it is difficult to speculate as to what the court might do to lose that influence. (The judiciary's allegedly central role in local party politics is an unconvincing explanation of the source of that authority.) It seems, however, that a too visible disregard for the (symbolic) authority of those on whom the court's own authority is dependent is an injudicious strategy. It is possible that the court misjudges its own authority and importance. It is remotely possible that the court's unwillingness to at least symbolically defer to the authority claims of others equally impressed with the importance of their own office may be the court's undoing. In a contest of wills between the juvenile court and other public officials, it is unclear where support for the court would originate.

Whatever the fate of the specific expectations of the provisions of the Juvenile Court Act discussed here, it is unlikely that the juvenile court will ever regain the unassailable position it once occupied in the legal, criminal-justice community. It is even possible that the Supreme Court decisions of the 1960s and the statutory reform of the 1970s are merely the initial steps culminating ultimately in a radical transformation of the juvenile court.

Continued dissatisfaction and criticism of the court's functioning can be expected to bring further judicial, legislative, and administrative attention to the court. Whether or not this attention results in more than cosmetic alterations will depend on the willingness and ability of other government entities to engage in oversight and enforcement tasks relative to juvenile-court compliance.

It has already been suggested that the infusion of new personnel into the juvenile court may bring a gradual transformation of behavior. Juvenile-court probation officers trained in criminal justice rather than social work might bring a more legalistic perspective to the activities of the juvenile court. My experience, however, with young probation officers with degrees in both social work and criminal justice suggests that staff attitudes and acknowledged practices are not perceptibly different between the two groups. If pressed to speculate about differences in the orientation of the two groups, different perspectives regarding crime control may be more easily hypothesized than are dissimilar notions of compliance, rule of law, or due process. It is unlikely that internal momentum for change will come from either of these groups.

Stapleton and Teitlebaum (1973) attribute much of the difference in rates of compliance to the judge's length of service on the juvenile-court bench. It is reasonable to assume that court behavior will become increasingly more compatible with the provisions of the Juvenile Court Act as new judges take the bench. To label such gradual, evolutionary accommodation as compliance, however, does some violence to the term as it is generally understood. It may be literally correct to refer to such quasi-voluntary accommodation to the expectation of law as compliance. It is more common and more theoretically and programmatically interesting, however, to suppose that the expectation to comply is less leisurely and more immediate, less voluntary and more coercive than this judicial-succession hypothesis suggests. If a less evolutionary image of court compliance is entertained, the motivation for such compliance must be expected to originate external to the juvenile court.

Neither legislative oversight, judicial review nor the activities of the Juvenile Court Judges Commission or the Department of Public Welfare have required the juvenile court to comply. The stance of any or all of these external actors could obviously change. What is not the least bit obvious is why inducements to comply have not previously been forthcoming or what might motivate these actors to demand compliance in the future.

The staff of the Juvenile Court Judges Commission are dependent on the goodwill of the juvenile-court judges. The commission staff is, however, administratively housed in the justice department in a larger research and planning unit. Commission staff have little or no involvement in the day-to-day activities of the juvenile court; their orientation and professional identification apparently is moving progressively toward a larger research and academic community. Staff members' credibility as researchers suffers both from the inaccuracy of that data provided them by the county courts and the limited uses to which that data is currently put. As the autonomy of this staff from the juvenile court grows, so may their demands for more accurate and extensive data. Although the commission staff may have no motivation to embarrass the court, more accurate and ambitious research would undoubtedly have that result. I believe that it will be the least likely of the four external units, the Juvenile Court Judges Commission, who will become the source of considerable, indirect pressure to comply.

Since the late 1960s the courts have heard many juvenile-court cases. Frequently decisions were rendered that suggest substantial change in juvenile-court practice. Courts that have seen fit to extend new rights to subjects of juvenile-court proceedings might be expected to protect those rights that are created by statute. I have been unable to determine whether or not appellate courts have circumvented issues of compliance or whether the absence of decisions in this area is attributable to the absence of cases on the grounds coming before them. The absence of counsel in the juvenile court and the dangers of appeal in the proceedings lend support to the latter explanation. Interviews with juvenile-court defense counsel elicited isolated examples suggesting the former hypothesis. Those lawyers who were interviewed were reluctant to believe that the appellate courts were willing to challenge the juvenile court regarding the provisions of the Juvenile Court Act. Such an opinion, regardless of its accuracy, would almost necessarily decrease the number of cases reaching appellate courts. For whatever reason, it is clear that appellate review has had little effect on compliance. Surely technical compliance would be achieved rapidly in the face of appellate insistence. Given the absence of adversarily orientated defense counsel or any other party willing and able to bring the issue of compliance to the court's attention, there is little reason to believe that appellate courts will become an obstacle to juvenile-court noncompliance.

Although I am not overly enthusiastic about the general usefulness of the ombudsman function, some readers may wish to consider the potential role of an ombudsman for obtaining compliance. If it is true that lawyers avoid the juvenile court or adversarial tactics because of the potential negative consequences such a stance might have for their client, an ombudsman may do safely what a lawyer is unable to do. Speaking for the state rather than for an individual client, the ombudsman could object to detention practices, the absence of required hearings, and so forth using statistics rather than individual cases. The ombudsman, unlike the lawyer, would also have the authority to attempt to activate those enforcement resources in state government that could motivate compliance.

The Department of Public Welfare has been identified as the public organization that might be expected to regulate or monitor the behavior of the juvenile court. The department has completely abdicated whatever responsibility it might have in this area. It has not produced a very impressive record of monitoring any of the human-service delivery systems over which it has administrative and fiscal authority. Perhaps the general unpopularity of the welfare function places the Department of Public Welfare in a particularly cautious and defensive stance relative to its environment. Whatever the motivation for its insecurity, it has always been careful lest it offend or cause controversy. Since it is the administrative mechanism of government that must ultimately assume enforcement and regulatory responsibility and since the Department of Public Welfare is the administrative entity responsible for treatment afforded juveniles, there is currently little justification for presuming that the state will demand compliance of the juvenile court.

The 1977 amendments to the Juvenile Court Act do, however, more specifically oblige the Department of Public Welfare to assume a more dominant role in administering the provision of services to juveniles. The department's authority over juvenile detention centers is much clearer than with respect to juveniles detained in county jails. The 1977 amendments forbade the use of county jails for detention after 31 December 1979. It also instructed the Department of Public Welfare to "take whatever steps it deems necessary to provide the required detention services" for any county that failed to submit plans for the removal of juveniles from adult facilities by 31 December 1978. Also, the department is permitted to refuse custody of juveniles in institutions which are at 110 percent of their stated capacity and to initiate transfer of youth institutionalized by the court. In all, the 1977 amendments provide the Department of Public Welfare with greater real and symbolic authority relative to juvenile-court functions. The opportunity to more aggressively regulate the behavior of the juvenile court is clearly provided, however, its previous record suggests that the opportunity will not be taken. If an administrative organization is to be expected to bring pressure on the juvenile court to comply, it is unlikely that the Department of Public Welfare will be that organization.

Recent federal legislation has provided a monitoring quasi-regulatory agency. In 1974 the Bayh Act (Public Law 93-145) became law. Although no immediate obligations on the state juvenile court resulted, the provisions of the act envisioned rather dramatic changes for the near future. Of particular relevance to the state courts were the expectations that criminal offenders—juveniles guilty of offenses that would be criminal if committed by an adult—be detained and institutionalized separately from status offenders and non-offenders—children alleged or found to be deprived, neglected, or dependent. Federal funds are made available to the states for the provision of shelter-care facilities for the detention of status offenders and non-offenders. Receipt of these and other Bayh Act funds are contingent on compliance with these expectations. In addition, funding is contingent on a system of monitoring and inspection of state juvenile facilities. Although monitoring and inspection are not defined and the federal agency responsible for administering the provisions of the act immediately expressed its willingness to allow a substantial period of time for compliance, the monitoring-and-inspection activity represents a potential challenge to the court's discretionary power. The monitoring and inspection must be done on an on-site basis precluding--ostensibly--the use of data supplied by the juvenile courts for that purpose. Clearly the impact of this function will be determined by the interpretation of the regulatory aggressiveness intended in the monitoring-and-inspection mission by federal program administrators and the agency delegated to monitoring-and-inspection functions in each state. At least in conventional usage, however, the terms monitoring and inspection imply judgmental oversight, concern with compliance, and the prospect of negative sanction, that is, failure to pass inspection presupposes a penalty.

Although the data reported in chapter 4 was obtained as a result of a monitoring-and-inspection effort undertaken at the insistence of the then commissioner of youth of the Department of Public Welfare, it is interesting that the timidity of that study falls well short of what might generally be held to be monitoring and inspection and that subsequent studies were not undertaken for 1976 or 1977. The failure has not resulted in state disqualification for receipt of federal juvenile-delinquency funds. It appears that federal administrative officials, like state officials, have defined their role as one that does not involve oversight or regulatory-type functions relative to the juvenile court's compliance with either state or federal law.

The juvenile court has failed to comply with the provisions of the Juvenile Court Act not because of any necessary commitment by the court to previous practice but because compliance was never demanded (or even suggested) by other actors in the juvenile justice system. The reason for the silence of other affected parties is far from clear. Pennsylvania Juvenile Court judges have historically had more power than juvenile judges in most other jurisdictions. Pennsylvania judges have had full authority over institutional commitments, release dates, and other elements of the processing of juveniles that frequently are the responsibility of other governmental entities in other states. It is uncertain whether or not juvenile-court judges view their power as essentially unlimited, however, there is every indication that other public actors are of this opinion. Even public officials who were quite critical of juvenile-court practice—at least with specific practices—spoke as though they were unable to act. Those questioned, particularly in the Department of Public Welfare, seemed to be convinced that the juvenile-court judges possessed some massive retaliatory ability that they would engage were their authority questioned. Officials talked as though it was suicidal to antagonize the court. It was never clear, however, exactly what the source or nature of this alleged power was thought to be. Because no one expected compliance, there is little reason for surprise that it was not forthcoming.

In the absence of even techical compliance, neither substantial compliance nor impact has been (or could have been) considered. Technical compliance could have been achieved had it been demanded by the juvenile-justice actors. The impact of such compliance is uncertain. It would seem that, over the short term, it would be minimal; but compliance would nevertheless be functional in precipitating further restructuring of the juvenile justice system over the long run. Noncompliance with both *Gault* and the Juvenile Court Act is particularly inhibitive of further appellate review of juvenile-court behavior. There is reason to believe that the examination of the relationship between legislative judicial, and administrative responses to noncompliance—particularly if one considers substantial compliance or impact—is essential to an understanding of why compliance is or is not obtained. In the Pennsylvania Juvenile Court the prospects for compliance are dependent on externally imposed demands for compliance. Under normal circumstances these demands would be expected to come from the administrative and judicial branches of government. Why, when, how, and under what circumstances these demands will be imposed are questions beyond the scope of this book.

Discretion and Compliance: The Direction of Future Research

Concern about discretion and compliance has only recently occasioned ambitious and specific social scientific inquiry. The first major work dealing with discretion (Davis 1970) remains, despite its shortcomings, the most significant treatment of the topic to date. Wasby (1970) occupies a similar status with respect to the compliance literature. The relative newness of these topics reveals a significant fact. Journalists, academics, politicians, and most of the lay public have frequently asked and volunteered answers to the question of why individuals violate the law. The answers remain relatively unsatisfactory, although they have been offered profusely for some time. And obviously, should a public official take a bribe, engage in fraud, or otherwise violate the criminal law, there are those who profess outrage and indignation (though less aggressively than if the perpetrator had been a welfare recipient engaged in fraud). For reasons that are difficult to understand, violations of adminstrative law by public entities are received quite differently. Administrative law tacitly assumes compliance since no penalties are envisioned should it be violated. Academics refer to governmental violations of the law not as "lawlessness" but as discretion or noncompliance. With few, isolated, and esoteric exceptions the legal and social-science professions have expended little effort in the examination of mechanisms by which government seeks to regulate itself or of the effectiveness with which this regulation is achieved. As a society, we are even less interested.

In a very real sense, the speculations entertained in this and the previous chapter may be read as an attempt to generate a theory of deterrence. Deterrence theory has not faired particularly well in criminology despite the recent resurgence of interest. Classical criminology based its reliance on deterrence on the assumption that law violation was a rational choice elected among competing alternatives. While such an assumption is singularly unconvincing with respect to crimes of passion, it has a ring of authenticity when applied to areas such as income-tax and motor-vehicle violations. In these latter instances it is reasonable to suggest that violators rationally calculate the potential advantages and disadvantages of compliance. It may be profitable to assume, at least tentatively, the rationality of organizational behavior. Such an assumption is warranted when, as is the case with most compliance studies, noncompliance is the norm rather than the exception. Were noncompliance the statistically deviant response, there might then be reason to entertain more individual, situational, and nonrational explanatory hypotheses. In addition, an examination of the situations considered thus far by the compliance literature suggest that the rational interest mitigating toward noncompliance need not be too powerful since negative consequences are essentially absent. This book has essentially explained juvenile-court noncompliance as resulting from the absence of any externally imposed inducement to comply. Neither the law itself nor other affected units of government behave in a manner reasonably calculated to deter noncompliance. Earlier studies of noncompliance focused attention on reasons for noncompliance. This book has examined the absence of reasons to comply. It has focused on enforcement, regulation, oversight, and penalties and calls for a type of analysis very similar to that suggested by deterrence theory in criminology.

In addition to the need to understand the factors that motivate or coerce compliance (or require officials to limit their decisional options to those permitted by law), there are numerous other problems involving the study of discretion and compliance that demand further attention. More thoughtful and rigorous theoretical and research efforts relative to these issues will be necessary if discretion and compliance—in fact governmental behavior itself—is to be understood.

Definitional Clarity

There is a sense in which the contemporary usage of the terms discretion and compliance is both too narrow and too broad. It is too broad in that it permits substantially different behaviors or conditions to be subsumed under the same headings. Discretion is used to refer to decision making within and beyond legally imposed bounds and even to decisions that are more restricted than the options permitted or anticipated by law (that is, the imposition of uniform sentences or bail where statutes anticipate individualization). In all conventional usage and in much of the academic literature, the term discretion is employed so casually as to render it meaningless and/or misleading. Usually it means nothing more than official decision making. Under such circumstances there is reason to fear that the term obscures more than it clarifies; that it evokes a sense of definitional precision that is absent from most discussions. Those who admire linguistic precision might be well advised to avoid the term altogether. The distinction made here between discretionary authority and discretionary power, though clumsy, is a useful but not sufficient clarification. The term retains a disturbing vacuity.

By contrast, the term *compliance* has a meaning that is relatively clear and uncontaminated. The difficulty lies less in its meaning than in its application. In the example of the Juvenile Court Act, there is little ambiguity regarding technical compliance. Substantial compliance or even technical compliance with reference to more vaguely, imprecisely worded legislation or court decisions, however, presents problems. Any assessment of substantial compliance ultimately rests on the assessor's assumptions regarding the intention of others. Even when one has been a party to a collective decision, it is frequently obvious that proposals are accepted for quite diverse motives and on the basis of markedly differing assumptions (or intentions) regarding impact. This unavoidable uncertainty with respect to intention often leads to a situation in which the wishes of the commentator—rather than the legislature or the court—form the basis for evaluation. Phrases such as "all deliberate speed" and "maximum feasible participation" or "fundamental fairness" invite this type of confusion. Even such apparently straight-forward, self-defining terms as *desegregation* or even *hearing* inevitably invite discord.

The problem of determining intent is so monumental that the term *impact* becomes an increasingly attractive alternative to compliance. For many purposes such a solution is appropriate and informative. For those interested in the control, regulation, and structuring of official decision making, however, it is no solution at all. Control or regulation necessarily assumes intentionality. Therefore a definition of compliance that accounts for judicial or legislative intent is required.

There is an equally troubling sense in which the terms discretion and compliance are used in a too narrow, restricted manner. Considerable effort has been devoted to specifying the nature of the relationship between discretion and compliance. It has been maintained that in some situations interest in discretion is indistinguishable from interest in compliance. Discussions of one of these terms do not acknowledge the relevance of the other. Were this unacknowledged similarity restricted to only these two terms, the issue would be trivial and easily resolved. However, there are numerous terms, phrases, and areas of study currently in vogue that bear an intimate relationship to compliance and discretion. In what ways, for instance, are compliance and implementation studies obliged to develop along separate paths? What is the relationship between concerns about accountability or responsiveness and discretion or compliance? Is not the alleged growth of administrative law and interest in regulatory administration related to a mounting awareness of problems associated with discretion and compliance. Is not the growing interest in ombudsman or ombudsman-type functions a tacit acknowledgment of the reluctance of public officials to voluntarily monitor their own discretionary decision-making and comply with the formal expectations of law? These currently popular topics show an obvious concern with regulating, controlling, or monitoring official public behavior. They are treated, however, as separate and discrete areas of study: Little effort has been expended to examine commonalities among them or construct a general theory of governmental regulation. There is every reason to believe that the sophistication of each of these interest areas would be enhanced were they better informed of the theoretical and research contributions of the other. In this sense current scholarly effort is too narrowly focused, resulting in the development of numerous subdisciplines for essentially the same or closely related phenomena.

Organizational and Environmental Factors

Much has already been said here about the overemphasis on personal characteristics of subjects and decision makers in the discretion and the compliance literature. This is not to suggest that such factors do not often have an impact. In the juvenile courts studied, for example, only two counties made extensive use of weekend detention as a sentence. Several counties routinely detained juveniles for probation violations; most never did so. Rates of detention, behaviors for which juveniles were detained, delegation of authority to order detention, rates of juveniles institutionalized or detained, relative length of confinement for status and criminal offenders, and numerous other practices varied markedly from county to county. It would be foolish to suggest that many of these differences are not to be accounted for by personal or philosophical characteristics of the various juvenile courts. Some variation may also result from differences in local political attitudes, racial, ethnic, or class composition of jurisdictions, community sentiments toward criminality, or economic factors. The research reported here provides ample evidence of numerous local and personal idiosyncracies of the Pennsylvania Juvenile Court. Were noncompliance or probable instances of abuse of discretion isolated or sporadic phenomena, personal or situational factors might form the basis for acceptable explanatory hypotheses. Even here, however, questions regarding the nature and absence of organizational or environmental reaction to such occurrences inevitably arise. Neither broad discretionary power nor noncompliance are statistically deviant incidents in the Pennsylvania Juvenile Court, however, they are pervasive throughout the system. This also is the case in those other areas in which discretion and compliance have been studied. Under such circumstances, systematic and environmental factors offer the only satisfactory explanation.

Strategies for Reducing Discretion

Davis (1969, 1974, 1975) and Reich (1963, 1964, 1965) have been identified as the major theoretical proponents of strategies for reducing or controlling the decisional authority and power of public officials. These proposals would be equally useful if applied as strategies to coerce or induce compliance. Davis sees the solution in administrative rule making; Reich advocates the development of rights and protections through adjudication. Perhaps because of a desire not to be identified with the overzealous proposals of earlier rule-of-law advocates or due to contempt for the competence, motivation, and power of the legislature, those advocating reduced discretion have had little to say about the role of the legislative process.

Two objections are offered. First, the issue is currently debated as though it were an either-or problem. It is more profitable to consider the relationship between legislative, judicial, and administrative activity. The successful reduction of discretion or encouragement of compliance is likely only if there is support from at least one other branch of government. For instance, the involvement of federal administrative officials, primarily from HEW, added an important dimension to school desegration (compliance with *Brown* v. *Board of Education*) and equal rights (compliance with the Civil Rights Act). It seems that the nature of administrative response is central to compliance.

The foregoing discussion would appear to lend support to the Davis hypothesis regarding administrative rule making. But this leads to the second objection. The administrative rule-making hypothesis assumes that it will be the rule making of the affected office that accomplishes the reduction of discretion. Although the concern here is with the juvenile court, courts have administrative as well as judicial functions. In this context rule or policy making by the Juvenile Court Judges Commission would meet all of the definitional requirements of administrative rule making. Attention has been focused, however, on the administrative response of organizations other than the ones affected. Regulation is anticipated from the external interorganizational environment rather than from the organization itself. Focusing attention on enforcement, deterrence, and regulation, the analytical framework suggested here sees the interactions, interdependencies, and distribution of resources among governmental agencies as critical to an understanding of discretion and compliance. The administrative response or rule making of other administrative agencies demands attention.

Speculative Hypotheses

There are certain assumptions and ideas that have fascinated me throughout the research that elude consideration in a manner permitting integration with the other material. They are presented here serially without any attempt to relate them to issues previously discussed. These topics are roughly ordered in terms of my assumptions about their potential utility.

The nature of assumptions about cause-and-effect knowledge must inevitably have an impact both on the attractiveness of discretion—including discretionary power or noncompliance—to the decision maker and the willingness of others to delegate or permit broad discretionary authority or tolerate noncompliance. If an undesirable condition is believed to result from the quality of a identifiable decision, I am convinced that most decision makers—public officials or others—will first attempt to avoid responsibility for that decision; failing that, they will meticulously structure their decision so that they are protected by the rules of the organization. The organizational literature, which attends to the dysfunctional aspects of bureaucracy, has much to say about official behavior that results from such decisional circumstances. Recall the earlier example of the decision to release a juvenile from detention in which the offender again engages in a visible violation of law. The decision to release is immediately seen as inappropriate. The violation is seen as proof of this inadequacy. There is no comparable proof of the inadequacy of a decision to continue detention. In juvenile justice, criminal justice, and the human services generally, it is often difficult to identify with any particularity what an achievable (positive) outcome might be, let alone identify the specific decision point(s) on which achievement rests. Under such circumstances one would expect considerable discretion to be permitted and exercised since the absence of positive outcome will not become the responsibility of the decision maker. There is every reason to believe that the nature of assessment that is, or can be, employed has a considerable impact on official discretion.

It is currently fashionable to bemoan the inappropriateness of rules. While a careful analysis of most discussions will discover that it is the content of rules that is being objected to, the discussion nonetheless leaves the impression that it is rules themselves that are objectionable. I am unaware of a truly commendable discussion of the role, function, and utility of rules. There is a more than necessary amount of confusion regarding this issue, but I have trouble suggesting ways to clarify this situation. Several specific correctives to what appears to be contemporary thinking are offered, however.

1. There are apparently many people who will only be satisfied with a rule under conditions of full knowledge of cause and effect and full or near full consensus regarding desired outcomes. While rules under such conditions would certainly be acceptable, they would also be trivial since appropriate behavior would be known without the assistance of rules. What is frequently overlooked is the necessity of rules in situations where the rules are arbitrary. Rules regarding time are excellent examples. It is preposterous to suggest that seventy-two hours is the optimum, or even the appropriate maximum, time for a juvenile detention-hearing. The 180-day rule and rules regarding the execution or contesting of contracts are similar examples. It would be even more

preposterous to suggest that such decisions may reasonably be made on an individual basis. Since what is just or appropriate is unknowable, a preestablished, arbitrary rule is absolutely necessary. For instance, the pernicious heritage of the rehabilitative ideal is that it has fostered faith in both the identification and the attainment of desirable individual solutions. There is reason to believe, however, that in many decision situations only arbitrary general rules will suffice because desired interventions and outcomes are unknown and unknowable.

2. At least in discussions with university students, one gets the sense that the only function of rules is to foreclose positive alternatives. For them as individuals they may frequently be correct. The fact that they are at a university suggests that social institutions have treated them fairly well, and there is reason to believe that this beneficent treatment will, in general, continue. But this privileged status leads to a myopic naivete. When the student objects to a preestablished formal grading formula without allowances for individual assessment, he assumes that his "C" grade would become an "A" or a "B" if the instructor had evaluated him on more personal, individualized criteria. That it never occurs to him that a "D" or an "F" are also possibilities under such a grading scheme is obvious. The assumption of the beneficent motives of high-school and university teachers to "good," middle-class students is not too problematic; in fact, it may be a reasonable assumption regarding most of the organizational actors with whom the more privileged members of society interact. It seems singularly unwarranted, however, to extend such an assumption to the motives of those interacting with the subjects of juvenile justice, adult criminal-justice, social welfare, and mental health. While rules may often serve to protect organizations from legitimate demands from their subjects, they may also serve to protect subjects from the illegitimate demands of otherwise omnipotent social institutions. It is this function of rules that is frequently overlooked.

3. Ultimately one resolves the debate between discretion and rule of law—for oneself at least—through a prioritizing of distrusts. Legislatures, courts, and administrative entities may make formal, universally applicable rules that will be almost guaranteed to be less than satisfactory in many respects. The question becomes whether or not one would prefer to entrust to the competency, the benign motivation, and the good faith of individual officials the responsibility of

arriving at more satisfactory behavior, absent external guidance and control. To the cynic, the alternatives are dismal; but history suggests that a too optimistic endorsement of either alternative is naive.

Much has been said here about reducing discretion. There is reason to believe that many proposals for reducing discretion will inevitably lead only to a relocation of the discretionary prerogative. There is little reason to quarrel with such a suggestion, particularly since numerous examples can be cited where that appears to have happened. Because it has happened, however, does not mean it has always or will always happen. Certainly total system reduction of discretion is a possibility, even though there may always be some informal reshuffling of discretion within the system. There may be an irreducible minimum of discretion necessary to system functioning; it is unwarranted to suggest that any governmental entity in the United States has yet approached that point.

Those who would study discretion, however, should be continually cautious lest they confuse reduced discretion with the relocation of discretionary decision making. The strategist may also be advised to consider estimation of the most desirable point for the exercise of discretion and advocate proposals calculated to encourage relocation to that point. In many situations the point at which discretion is exercised, the visibility of that decision point, and the access to formal or informal review at that point may be a more significant issue than the estimate of the aggregate amount of discretion within a system.

Bibliography

Allen, Francis A. 1959. "Criminal Justice, Legal Values, and the Rehabilitative Ideal." *Journal of Criminal Law, Criminology and Police Science* 50(September-October):226.

Ares, Charles E., Rankin, Anne, and Stuez, Herbert. 1963. "Manhattan Bail Project: An Interim Report on the Use of Pre-trial Parole." *New York University Law Review* 38(January):67.

Becker, Theodore L., and Feeley, Malcolm M. 1973. *The Impact of Supreme Court Decisions.* New York: Oxford University Press.

Becker, Theodore L., and Murray Vernon G., eds. 1971. *Government Lawlessness in America.* New York: Oxford University Press.

Birkby, Robert H. 1966. "The Supreme Court and the Bible Belt: Tennessee Reaction to the 'Schempp' Decision." *Midwest Journal of Political Science* 10(August):304-315.

Black, Donald J. 1970. "Production of Crime Rates." *American Sociological Review* 35(August):733-747.

Black, Donald J., and Reiss, Albert J., Jr. 1970. "Police Control of Juveniles." *American Sociological Review* 35(February):63-77.

Blaustein, Albert P., and Furgason, Clarence, Jr. 1957. *Desegregation and the Law.* New Brunswick, N.J.: Rutgers University Press.

Boles, Daniel F. 1965. *The Bible, Religion and the Public Schools.* Ames, Iowa: Iowa State University Press.

Bullock, Henry A. 1961. "Significance of the Racial Factor in the Length of Prison Sentences." *Journal of Criminal Law, Criminology and Police Science* 52:411-417.

Canon, B.C., and Kolson, K. 1971. "Rural Compliance with Gault: Kentucky, A Case Study." *Journal of Family Law* 10:300.

Chambliss, William J. 1975. "Toward A Political Economy of Crime." *Theory and Society* 2(Summer):149-181.

Chambliss, William, and Nagasawa, Richard H. 1969. "On the Validity of Official Statistics: A Comparison Study of White, Black, and Japanese High School Boys." *Research in Crime and Delinquency* 6(January):71-77.

Cochran, Peggy. 1971. "A Situational Approach to the Study of Police-Negro Relations." *The Sociological Quarterly* 12(Spring): 232-237.

Cole, George F. 1975. *The American System of Criminal Justice*. North Scituate, Mass.: Duxbury Press.

Davis, James F. 1970. *Social Problems*. New York: Free Press.

Davis, Kenneth Culp. 1969. *Discretionary Justice*. Urbana: University of Illinois Press.

______ . 1974. "An Approach to Legal Control of the Police." *Texas Law Review* 52(April):703-725.

______ . *Police Discretion*. St. Paul: West Publishing.

______ . 1976. *Discretionary Justice in Europe and America*. Urbana: University of Illinois Press.

Dershowitz, Alan M. 1976. *Fair and Certain Punishment*. New York: McGraw-Hill.

Diamond, B.L. 1974. "The Psychiatric Prediction of Dangerousness." *University of Pennsylvania Law Review*, 123(December):439-452.

Dworkin, Ronald M. 1967. "The Model of Rules." *Yale Law Review* 35:14-46.

Edelman, Murray. 1977. *Political Language*. New York: Academic Press.

Eisenstein, James, and Jacob, Herbert. 1977. *Felony Justice: An Organizational Analysis of Criminal Courts*. Boston: Little, Brown.

Erikson, Kai T. 1966. *Wayward Puritans*. New York: John Wiley and Sons.

Fogel, David. 1975. *We Are the Living Proof*. Cincinnati: W.H. Anderson.

Fox, Sanford J. 1970. "Juvenile Justice Reform: An Historical Perspective." *Stanford Law Review* 22(June):1187.

______ . 1971. *The Law of Juvenile Courts in a Nutshell*. St. Paul: West Publishing.

Frankel, Marvin E. 1973. *Criminal Sentences*. New York: Hill and Wang.

Friedman, Lawrence. 1967. "Legal Rules and the Process of Social Change." *Stanford Law Review* 19(April):786.

Goffman, Erving. 1961. *Asylums*. Garden City, N.Y.: Doubleday.

Goldfarb, Ronald. 1965. *Ransom: A Critique of the American Bail System*. New York: Harper & Row.

Goldfarb, R.L., and Singer, L.R. 1970. "Redressing Prisoners Grievances." *George Washington Law Review* 39(December):175.

Goldman, Nathan. 1963. *The Differential Selection of Juvenile Offenders for Court Appearance*. New York: National Council on Crime and Delinquency.

Goldstein, Herman. 1967. "Administrative Problems in Controlling the Exercise of Police Discretion." *Journal of Criminal Law, Criminology and Police Science* 78(June):160.

Goldstein, Joseph. 1960. "Police Discretion Not to Invoke the Criminal Process." *Yale Law Journal* 69(March):543.

Green, Edward. 1961. *Judicial Attitudes in Sentencing*. London: Macmillan.

Hagen, John. 1974. "Extra-Legal Attributes and Criminal Sentencing: An Assessment of a Sociological Viewpoint." *Law and Society Review* 8(Spring):357-383.

Hermann, Joachim. 1976. "The German Prosecutor." In *Discretionary Justice in Europe and America*, edited by Kenneth Culp Davis, pp. 16-74. Urbana: University of Illinois Press.

Hill, Roscoe, and Feeley, Malcolm, eds. 1968. *Affirmative School Integration*. Beverly Hills: Sage Publications.

Hohenstein, William F. 1969. "Factors Influence the Police Disposition of Juvenile Offenders." In *Delinquency: Selected Studies*, edited by Thorsten Sellins and Marvin E. Wolfgang, pp. 138-149. New York: John Wiley and Sons.

Hutchins, Robert M. 1976. Foreword to *Pursuing Justice for the Child*, by Margaret K. Rosenheim. Chicago: University of Chicago Press.

James, Howard. 1970. *Children in Trouble: A National Scandal*. New York: McKay.

Johnson, Richard. 1967. *The Dynamics of Compliance*. Evanston, Ill.: Northwestern University Press.

Jones, Charles O. 1977. *An Introduction to the Study of Public Policy*. 2d ed. Belmont, Cal.: Wadsworth.

Jowell, Jeffrey L. 1975. *Law and Bureaucracy: Administrative Discretion and the Limits of Legal Action*. Cambridge, Mass.: Dunellen Publishing.

Kadish, Sanford. 1962. "Legal Norms and Discretion in the Police and Sentencing Process." *Harvard Law Review* 75(March):904.

Kast, F.E., and Rosenzweig, J.E. 1973. *Contingency Views of Organization and Management*. Chicago: Scientific Research Associates.

Kittrie, Nicholas N. 1971. *The Right to Be Different*, Baltimore: Johns Hopkins Press.

Krajick, Kevin, 1977. "A Step Toward Determinacy for Juveniles." *Corrections Magazine* (September):37-42.

Krislov, Samuel; Boyum, Keith O.; Clark, Jerry N.; Shaefer, Roger C.; and White, Susan O., eds. 1972. *Compliance and the Law*. Beverly Hills: Sage.

LaFave, Wayne R. 1962. "The Police and Non-Enforcement of the Law." *Wisconsin Law Review* 5:104-137.

______ . 1965. *Arrest: The Decision to Take a Suspect into Custody*. Boston: Little, Brown.

Lefstein, N., Stapleton V., and Teitelbaum L. 1969. "In Search of Juvenile Justice: Gault and Its Implementation." *Law & Society Review* 3(May):491.

Lemert, E.M. 1967. "Legislative Change in the Juvenile Court." *Wisconsin Law Review* (Spring):421.

Lindsey, B. 1904. "The Juvenile Court in Denver." In *Children's Courts in the United States*, edited by S. Borrows. Washington: U.S. Government Printing Office.

Medalie, Richard J., Zeitz, Leonard, and Alexander, Paul, 1968. "Custodial Police Interrogation in Our Nation's Capital: The Attempt to Implement Miranda." *Michigan Law Review* 66(May):1347-1422.

Miller, Jerome, and Ohlin, Lloyd E. 1976. "The New Corrections: The Case of Massachusetts." In *Pursuing Justice for the Child*, edited by Margaret K. Rosenheim. Chicago: University of Chicago Press.

Morris, Norval. 1974. "The Future of Imprisonment: Toward a Punitive Philosophy." *Michigan Law Review* 72(May):1161-1180.

Moynihan, Daniel P. 1969. *Maximum Feasible Misunderstanding*. New York: Free Press.

Muir, W. 1962. *Prayer in the Public Schools*. Chicago: University of Chicago Press.

Murphy, Walter F. 1959. "Lower Court Checks on Supreme Court Power." *American Political Science Review* 53(December): 1017-1031.

Neustadt, Richard E. 1960. *Presidential Power: The Politics of Leadership*. New York: John Wiley and Son.

Nonet, Phillippe. 1969. *Administrative Justice*. New York: Russell Sage.

Ohlin, Lloyd E., Coates, Robert B., and Miller, Alden D. 1974. "Radical Correctional Reform: A Case Study of the Massachusetts Youth Correctional System." *Harvard Educational Review* 44:74-111.

O'Leary, V., and Nuffield, J. 1972. "Parole Decision Making Characteristics." *Criminal Law Bulletin* 11(September-October): 555-586.

Packer, Herbert L. 1968. *The Limits of the Criminal Sanction*. Stanford: Stanford University Press.

Paulsen, Monrad. 1967. "The Constitutional Domestication of the Juvenile Court." *Supreme Court Review*, p. 233.

Pekelis, Alexander. 1950. *Law and Social Action: Selected Essays*. Edited by Milton R. Konvite. Ithaca: Cornell University Press.

Peltason, J.W. 1961. *Fifty-eight Lonely Men: Southern Federal Judges and School Desegration*. New York: Harcourt, Brace & World.

Pepinsky, Harold E. 1976. *Crime and Conflict*. New York: Academic Press.

Piliavin, Irving, and Briar, Scott. 1964. "Police Encounters with Juveniles." *American Journal of Sociology* 70(September): 206-214.

Perrow, Charles. 1970. *Organizational Analysis: A Sociological View*. Belmont, Cal.: Brooks/Cole.

Piven, Frances, and Cloward, Richard. 1971. *Regulating the Poor*. New York: Random House.

Platt, A., and Friedman, R. 1968. "The Limits of Advocacy: Occupational Hazards in Juvenile Court." *University of Pennsylvania Law Review* 116(May):1156.

Platt, Anthony. 1969. *The Child Savers: The Invention of Delinquency*. Chicago: University of Chicago Press.

Pound, Roscoe. 1937. Foreword to *Social Treatment in Probation and Delinquency*, by Pauline Young. New York: McGraw-Hill.

Pressman, Jeffrey L., and Wildavsky, Aaron B. 1973. *Implementation*. Berkeley: University of California Press.

Quinney, Richard. 1973. *Critique of the Legal Order*. Boston: Little, Brown.

Reich, Charles A. 1963. "Midnight Welfare Searches and the Social Security Act." *Yale Law Journal* 72(June):1347.

______ . 1964. "The New Property." *Yale Law Journal* 73(April): 773.

______ . 1965. "Individual Rights and Social Welfare: The Emerging Issues." *Yale Law Journal* 74(June):1245.

______ . 1966. "The Law of the Planned Society." *Yale Law Journal* 75(July):1227.

Rosenheim, Margaret. 1962. *Justice for the Child*. New York: Free Press.

Rothman, David. 1971. *The Discovery of the Asylum*. Boston: Little, Brown.

Rubenstein, Jonathan. 1973. *City Police*. New York: Farrar, Straus and Giroux.

Rutherford, Andrew. 1974. *The Dissolution of the Training Schools in Massachusetts*. Columbus, Ohio: Academy of Contemporary Problems.

Ryan, William. 1972. *Blaming the Victim*. New York: Vintage.

Sarratt, Reed. 1971. *The Ordeal of Desegregation: The First Decade*. New York: Macmillan.

Schlossman, Steven L. 1977. *Love and the American Delinquent*. Chicago: University of Chicago Press.

Seeburger, Richard H., and Wettick, R. Stanton, Jr. 1967. "Miranda in Pittsburgh: A Statistical Study." *University of Pittsburgh Law Review* 21(October):1.

Skolnick, Jerome H. 1966. *Justice without Trial: Law Enforcement in a Democratic Society*. New York: John Wiley and Sons.

Sprowls, James T., and Bullington, Bruce. 1976. "Removing Juveniles from Camp Hill: A Case Study." In *Juvenile Delinquency: Little Brother Grows Up*, edited by Theodore N. Ferdinand. Beverly Hills: Sage.

Stapleton, Von, and Teitlebaum, Lee. 1973. *In Defense of Youth: A Study of the Role of Counsel in American Juvenile Courts*. New York: Russell Sage.

Szasz, Thomas S. 1961. *The Myth of Mental Illness*. New York: Harper & Row.

______. 1963. *Law, Liberty, and Psychiatry*. New York: Macmillan.

______. 1970*a*. *Ideology and Insanity*. Garden City: Anchor.

______. 1970*b*. *The Manufacture of Madness*. New York: Dell Publishing.

Terry, Robert M. 1967. "The Screening of Juvenile Offenders." *Journal of Criminal Law, Criminology and Police Science* 58(June): 173-181.

Thompson, James D. 1967. *Organizations in Action*. New York: McGraw-Hill.

Thornberry, Terrence P. 1973. "Race, Socio-economic Status and Sentencing in the Juvenile Justice System." *Journal of Criminal Law and Criminology* 64(March):90-98.

Vines, Kenneth N. 1964. "Federal District Judges and Race Relations Cases in the South." *Journal of Politics* 26:337-357.

Von Hirsh, A. 1972. "Predictions of Criminal Conduct and Preventive Confinement of Convicted Persons." *Buffalo Law Review* 21(Spring):717.

______ . 1976. *Doing Justice: The Choice of Punishments.* New York: Hill and Wang.

Wasby, Stephen L. 1970. *The Impact of the United States Supreme Court.* Homewood, Ill.: Dorsey Press.

Westley, William A. 1970. *Violence and the Police: A Sociological Study of Law, Custom and Morality.* Cambridge, Mass.: MIT Press.

Wice, Paul B. 1973. "Bail Reform in American Cities." *Criminal Law Bulletin* 9(November):770-797.

Wick, William D. 1973. "Procedural Due Process in Disciplinary Hearings: The Case for Specific Constitutional Requirements." *South Dakota Law Review* 18:309.

Wilson, James Q. 1968. *Police Discretion.* Cambridge, Mass.: Harvard University Press.

Wolfgang, Marvin E. 1974. "Racial Discrimination in the Death Sentence." In *Executions in America,* edited by William J. Bowers. Lexington, Mass.: D.C. Heath, Lexington Books.

Yale Law Journal. 1967. "Interrogation in New Haven: The Impact of Miranda." *Yale Law Journal* 76:1519.

Index

Index

About the Author

James T. Sprowls received the Ph.D. in community systems planning and development from The Pennsylvania State University in 1979. Prior to that he taught community development and administration of justice at the university and worked on numerous research and demonstration projects in both adult and juvenile correctionals, social welfare, OIC, Upward Bound, and OEO community-action centers. He is currently an assistant professor of criminal justice in the School of Social Welfare at the University of Wisconsin—Milwaukee.